W9-BES-571

THE MAKING OF A
ROYAL MARINE
COMMANDO

THE MAKING OF A
ROYAL MARINE
COMMANDO

Nigel Foster

PRESIDIO

At the request of many Royal Marines themselves, this book is dedicated to their wives and families.

Acknowledgements

Too many members of the Royal Marines and Royal Navy have helped to be all mentioned by name . . . but those who were particularly helpful include: Nick Vaux, Robin Ross, Guy Liardet, Ian Moore, Tim Sloane, Mike Taffinder, Rob Ward, Chris Menhenniot, Paul Bancroft, Sandy Lade, Leo Williams, Ewan Southby Tailyour, Rob Need, Mark Spicer, Brian Wolvine, Dave Munelly, Pete Holdgate, Des Wassel, Fred Poyser, Pete Williams, Nigel Devenish, Nick Smith, Roger Ryan.

My particular thanks to: Recce Troop 42 Commando; Bravo Company 40 Commando; 539 Squadron; 3 Raiding Squadron; M&AW Cadre; SBS; Commando Training Centre, Lympstone; Royal Marines Poole; HMS *Intrepid*; HMS *Swallow*; and the Royal Netherlands Marine Corps.

Finally, thanks for all the hospitality shown me by various Officers' and Sergeants' Messes – and for some very memorable runs ashore, not forgetting the Ming Inn.

Page 1: The Commando Memorial at RM Lympstone
Frontispiece: Member of Recce Troop, 40 Commando
on a NATO exercise in Turkey

Published in the United States in 1988 by Presidio Press
31 Pamaron Way, Novato CA 94949

First published in Great Britain in 1987 by Sidgwick & Jackson Limited

Copyright © 1987 by Nigel Foster

Library of Congress Cataloging-in-Publication Data
Foster, Nigel.
  The making of a Royal Marine commando.
   1. Great Britain.   Royal Marines—Commando troops.
2. Commando troops.   I. Title.
VE57.F67   1988   359.9'6'0941   88–17989.

ISBN 0-89141-336-7

Designed by Paul Watkins

Phototypeset by Falcon Graphic Art Ltd
Wallington, Surrey
Printed in Great Britain by
Jolly & Barber Limited
for Sidgwick & Jackson Limited
1 Tavistock Chambers, Bloomsbury Way
London WC1A 2SG

CONTENTS

PREFACE

Major General Julian Thompson CB OBE

*As the Commanding Officer of 3 Commando Brigade RM,
both before and during the Falklands War, Julian Thompson
is credited with much of the successful planning and
execution of Operation Corporate that culminated in
the surrender of the Argentinian forces*

When Nigel Foster asked me to write a preface to his book, he was kind enough to mention that there had been some small disappointment in certain circles that he had not turned out a more 'authorized version'. I therefore awaited the proofs with some interest, particularly since he was brave (some would say foolhardy) enough to say that I should make whatever comments I liked.

This book is decidedly not the 'authorised version'! I would definitely take issue with certain of his comments and conclusions – not least those relating to comparisons between one fighting force and another, which to me have always been self-defeating. I would also be bound to say that the Scots Guards in particular did extremely well in the Falklands, facing as they did the best troops the Argentinians had available – the 5th Marine Battalion who were well dug in, fully alerted and prepared to fight it out.

But for me the real strength of Nigel Foster's book lies in the way he has succeeded in capturing the spirit of those incomparable soldiers: the Marines, Non-Commissioned Officers and Warrant Officers of the Royal Marines.

The general public will learn just what it takes to become a Royal Marine Commando. They will learn, as many an aspiring Commando has also learnt, that there are no short cuts – only mud, toil, sweat and sometimes, a few tears. For the true value of this book is that it shows the way in which one elite force is trained and motivated; and that it makes clear that the 'macho' culture so beloved of some TV and film producers does not impress anyone in the Royal Marines. 'Rambo' would last about ten minutes. And if the vivid way in which their training methods are described deters one 'Rambo' from joining the Corps, then Nigel Foster will have done the Royal Marines a service.

The training methods described *do* work. I happen to believe that they are the best; but then, like Nigel Foster, I am unashamedly biased.

JULIAN THOMPSON

Previous pages: Practising 'regains' over a water tank with dummy Lee Enfield rifles – real rifles can't take the same punishment as a recruit.
To do a 'regain', first crawl along a rope. Then swing off, hang down at full length supported by your hands. Then swing back up on to the rope. Then carry on crawling . . .

Right: Setting off on a modest 15-mile yomp, this 'Royal' carries an SMG (9mm), anti-tank rocket (66mm), spare ammo for both plus personal gear – a total of 120 pounds plus

Who are the Royal Marines, and why does any man want to become one?

The Royal Marines are an elite unit – however much they publicly deny it, preferring to refer to themselves as 'the thinking man's infantry'. They have, of course, a special responsibility for amphibious operations, and the responsibility for defending NATO's northern flank, with the result that the Royal Marines are *the* experts on Arctic survival and warfare.

Perhaps slightly disingenuously (in view of their very efficient PR organization), the Royal Marines (often abbreviated simply to 'Royal') take the attitude that since they, plus the powers that be, plus Britain's allies or potential enemies all know how effective the Corps is, there is little need for wholesale flag waving. They prefer to get on with the job, with the minimum of fuss and publicity. So when the old arguments are resurrected about the relative values of the Parachute Regiment, the French Foreign Legion, the United States Marine Corps (USMC), the French Paras, Belgian Paras, Soviet Guards, Soviet Spetznaz, the Gurkhas or whatever special elite unit is flavour of the month, the Royal Marines maintain a modest and becoming silence. Privately, they are under no illusion as to how good they are nor how good they need to be. Their status in the world league of elite forces can perhaps be judged by what other elite units think of them.

One of the more closely guarded secrets of the USMC is that the Royal Marines – both as a corps and as individuals – are held up to USMC recruits as the standard to aim for: 'One day, feller, if you're lucky and try real hard, you just might be as good as a Royal Marine.'

The Soviet Naval Infantry has, over the past fifteen years, reorganized itself to echo the Royal Marine role and training methods. And while the SNI's greater size and mechanization make it operationally more on a par with the USMC, it still sees its role as providing 'commando' troops. And it does, since the maritime element of the Soviet Union's Spetznaz troops is drawn from the SNI. It also stresses initiative far more than most other Soviet forces; and in terms of training, the SNI's Tower of Strength – a fifteen-metre-tall rope complex – is but an excellent variation of the famous (or infamous) Tarzan Course, at the Commando Training Centre,

Royal Marines, in Lympstone, South Devon. Imitation is indeed the sincerest form of flattery.

A British Para Officer or NCO would probably admit that the Paras would rather serve alongside the Royal Marines than with any other unit in the British armed forces.

Within the marine corps of the world, the Royal Marines set the standard not only because they are the oldest, but because they are the most experienced and successful. One cannot say of the Marines, as has been said of the SAS, that they don't admit their mistakes, but merely bury them.

That the Corps is an elite owes much to the twin traditions and roles of being both sea soldiers (Royal Marines) and Special Forces (Commandos). Marines (and this is taken from the Soviet definition, which holds good for all good marine units) must get used to long periods of danger and discomfort because they spend such long periods at sea in far from ideal conditions. A Marine must be able to go into action at a moment's notice, undertaking a variety of tasks from establishing a beachhead in unknown territory, to capturing a port or mounting raids and diversionary operations.

Dressed in blues and pith helmets, officers and men of 42 Commando mount guard at Buckingham Palace – the first of the British Armed Forces to do so with the new SA80 rifle

A commando must be able to operate independently for long periods and in extremely small groups. He must be able to move fast and hit hard; his training will emphasize the qualities of initiative, imagination and bravery. Both marines and commandos must be able to maintain their fighting edge in the face of atrocious conditions and morale-sapping changes of fortunes.

Any soldier can be trained up to the peak of physical fitness. Any soldier's military standards can (in theory, anyway) be raised to the standards of, say, the Special Air Service (SAS). But what marks the truly elite soldier is not his physcial ability or his skill at arms. It is his mental attitude, not only to war, but to life in general. As individuals, elite soldiers are extremely self-sufficient and independent. They tend to be quiet, in the belief that they have little or nothing to prove. Theirs is a mental toughness that combines extreme pragmatism and a (sometimes annoying) stubbornness.

As a unit, elite soldiers can rely on each other to a far greater extent than in more conventional units. They are aware of each other's abilities and the very intensity of their training fosters a family atmosphere. The Royal Marines, for example, are loyal to the Corps because the Corps is composed of Royal Marines – loyalty to other members often outweighs loyalty to an institution or abstract ideal.

All this is overlaid with a professionalism that demands the job to be done as quickly, as efficiently and as completely as possible. Elite troops are not known for half-measures, either on or off the battlefield.

The Commando role

That the Royal Marines are also commandos owes much to the fact that Britain's commandos can only be seaborne or airborne; and that the Royal Marines took the seaborne role for themselves in the Second World War – partly at the instigation of Lord Louis Mountbatten, who could point to a number of successful 'commando-style' operations that the Royal Marines had undertaken over the past 300 years. So it was that although the initial commando units in the Secord World War were composed of army personnel, the Royal Marines had made this their exclusive preserve by 1944. And in 1946 the Corps became responsible for all Britain's commando operations.

Today the Corps numbers some seven thousand men. The main striking force is 3 Commando Brigade, which has under its command 40, 42 and 45 Commando (a commando unit of approximately seven hundred men is equivalent to an army battalion). The rest of the Corps is split between various training establishments, headquarters staffs and units like the Special Boat Service (SBS) or Comacchio Group, neither of which come under the brigade for administrative purposes. The Corps also provides ships' detachments for the Royal Navy – which they have done since being first formed in 1664, one of their main tasks being (then) to prevent the crew from killing their officers, as well as providing Naval landing parties.

'If there's one thing more dangerous than an officer with a map,' commented a Royal Marine senior NCO, 'it's a matelot [Royal Navy sailor] with a gun.'

Amphibiosity

It's probably a good idea at this point to take a short detour and explain to the uninitiated what amphibious operations are, and why they're still regarded as being so important, despite the lack of empire and far-flung possessions. 'Amphibiosity' is an ugly word, but one that's often heard within the Ministry of Defence. It refers not only to the method of moving fighting men by ship, but also to a political and strategic doctrine.

Britain can only move troops out of the country by air or by sea. Airlifts are both vulnerable and final. If, for example, it ever became necessary to reinforce Norway because of rising political tension between NATO and the Warsaw Pact, a sudden airlift into that country would only add to the tension. More to the point, there are only a few airfields available in any country, any one of which can be easily sabotaged. Troop air transports are also extremely vulnerable to low-level rocket attack when coming in to land. However, a naval amphibious task force can effectively stooge around offshore, making its presence felt, without worsening the situation to any great degree. If it does have to land, it can do so at a time and a place of its own choosing. So amphibiosity allows great flexibility to politicians and military commanders alike. However, amphibious operations do require troops trained for the job. It is no easy matter to disembark soldiers at the best of times let alone in the depths of an arctic winter. If nothing else, the Falklands War proved that conventionally trained troops are simply not good enough.

However strategically vital it is, amphibiosity is probably not enough in itself to justify the continuing existence of the Royal Marines, which is why the Corps also undertakes a variety of more conventional roles, ranging from Northern Ireland to mounting guard outside Buckingham Palace. Of the two, they would probably prefer to be judged by their record in Northern Ireland. Anyone can mount guard outside Buck House.

The reason why

The Corps does not lack volunteers. Over the past ten years alone more than fifty thousand men have applied to join the Royal Marines. Of these, less than half have been accepted for a Potential Officer's Course (POC) or Potential Recruit's Course (PRC). Of these, less than a quarter have been accepted for training. And of these, less than sixty per cent have managed to win a Green Beret – the headgear that marks a man as a Commando, rather than a Royal Marine.

While a family military background can play a part in a man wanting to be a Royal Marine, it's by no means the only reason. After all, since the demise of National Service, there are far fewer parents and relatives who have any direct military experience.

One officer told how he'd 'sort of drifted' into the Corps while still at university. Something of a radical to begin with, he'd become disenchanted with student politics ('too much time and money spent writing letters of solidarity and attending conferences that never achieved anything; too little thought for student welfare – like proper accommodation or the price of beer in the Union bar'). He'd met a few Royal Marine Reservists through playing rugby ('very unradical that – playing rugby')

Keeping your weapon dry. Bravo Company, 40 Commando in Turkey during a NATO exercise. They deploy from the LCVP in strict formation – anti-tank rocket and machine gun on opposite flanks. Even in the water they spread out – the second rule is 'don't bunch!' Centre foreground is a radio operator from 59 Commando Regt Royal Engineers

and had visited them on their training nights – as much out of idle curiosity, or even morbid interest. But he found himself drawn more and more to the life, particularly its outdoor aspects, joined the Reserve and, when he discovered that the Corps would pay for the rest of his time at university, joined up. Somehow, he said, he'd felt that he had come home.

Another Marine, a recruit, remembered how he'd been running a successful transport business with his brother when he suddenly woke up one morning with the fixed determination to join the Marines – much to

his family's (and his own) surprise. The only reasons he could think of at the time were that he loved playing about in boats, that he felt there was more to life, that he wasn't being stretched or challenged enough – and that the Marines represented some sort of elite. 'I knew knack-all [nothing] about the Corps, can't really tell you why I joined. Anyway, that's not important – it's why you stay [in training] that counts.'

If there is a common factor, other than a sense of service, running through the motivations of those who want to be Royal Marines, it is possibly a feeling of wanting to be the best, of wanting to prove themselves: not so much for the opinions of others, not to impress family or friends, but simply to prove something to themselves. And it's sad but true that the majority of men who do join for the uniform, or out of bravado, will painfully discover in the first few weeks of training that there are easier ways of achieving the same objectives. There are also those who, having decided to join the armed forces, look around to see which service offers them the most. But again, this often comes back down to a basic desire to try for the one they see as being the toughest, with the accent on self-discovery. For many would-be Marines, it's also something they've always wanted to do, ever since boyhood. Quite how such a desire lasts throughout puberty and adolescence remains something of a mystery – unless the desire to be a Marine is as much a vocation as anything else. Certainly the training (and operational) demands on a Marine are tough enough to exclude all but the most determined.

Every now and then the odd psychopath attempts to join the Corps – as they do with the Paras, USMC or French Foreign Legion – attracted by what they see as a licence and opportunity to hurt people – by the power inherent in a gun. Men like these are not welcome and if by chance they get through the recruiting screens, the first month or so at Lympstone will find them out, and they will quietly be told to leave. Moral considerations aside, psychopaths do not make good soldiers, and definitely not good special forces. They don't respond well to discipline (and would be an extreme liability, say, on the streets of Belfast), tend to be egocentric to the point of unpleasant (and dangerous) selfishness, and contrary to the myth of the *Dirty Dozen*, psychopaths are not usually very courageous.

Of course the Corps teaches aggression; but it also teaches how to channel and control that aggression – how to use it only when it's absolutely necessary. Remoulding a warped character is not on the Lympstone curriculum.

Degrees of ability
At first sight the educational standards required of a potential Royal Marine are not exactly stringent. Five O levels, including Maths and English, plus two A levels are required for officers (the equivalent of a good high school diploma in North America). Recruits need to be able to read and write and to be numerate to a reasonable standard. All of this adds to the myth of the, well, slightly 'thick' Marine, who shouldn't be trusted with anything requiring too much brainpower.

It is a myth largely fostered by academics, piqued by the lack of recognition that they feel the Corps (and increasingly, the British Army) shows for their own intellectual disciplines and achievements. There is,

Real agony on the Potential Recruit's Course. Clockwise, from the top: Personal Admin during the two-week induction phase – not just bullshit, but teaching the need for extreme neatness and cleanliness when under pressure. If the lesson is learnt, it'll help keep them alive in war

Teaching recruits how to hang upside down on a rope using only their feet: it improves their agility and physical self-confidence

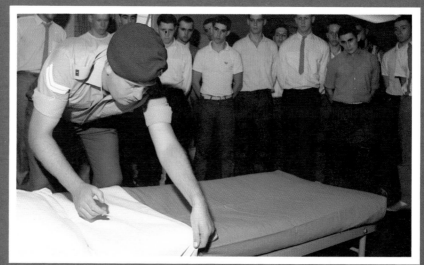

perhaps, the feeling that few if any of the men are capable of wielding great power and responsibility without the possession of a good honours degree.

The Royal Marines look at it slightly differently. They might, perhaps, point out that a junior officer – or a senior NCO – is trained to make the type of split-second analysis and decision that currency and commodity dealers have to make on the financial exchanges in London, New York, Chicago or Tokyo. A more senior officer is under the same stress as a director of a large company would be if he had to produce, day after day, the optimum business plan – and be able to change it at a moment's notice. There is the added pressure in both cases that if the soldier gets it wrong, he and his men will probably die, whereas the businessman will merely dust off his CV and go in search of a new job.

What this means in practice is that the Corps looks for intellectual potential and refuses to accept that an academic qualification always indicates that a man possesses it; nor that his intellect will hold up in times of stress. Yet, given that, the Marines do go to great lengths to recruit from the universities, for two reasons. First, in an attempt to get graduates possessing more practical degrees – a language, science or possibly engineering. Second, the Marines are well aware that the corridors of power are stalked by men and women who enjoy a similar academic background. It would be useful, the Corps possibly feels, that it should have senior officers who can reminisce about dreaming spires and May Balls with the best of them. Also, despite its reservations about purely academic abilities being relevant to a soldier's life, the Corps recognizes that some aspects of military planning do require extreme intellectual ability. At the same time, many officers say privately that any man who shows the potential can be trained and taught within the system; including being sent to university at a later date.

Feet in the right position – but too much weight is supported by arms and shoulders. He should be vertical, with thigh and stomach muscles sharing the load. And by tomorrow, he probably will be

Classless society

If there is one quality that the Royal Marines do look for, it is street sense – possibly best described as common sense with an edge. It cannot be taught, although it can be developed. If it doesn't exist in the first instance, it never will, at least not to the level required. It is, however, something that can perhaps best be stimulated by the company of one's fellow would-be Marines – and is one of the reasons why the Corps does try to recruit as many officers as it can from the state school system. Having said that, over fifty per cent of all potential officers do come from the independent-school sector – largely because they show an earlier-developed sense of responsibility and integrity, plus ambition and a good intellectual background – they have, hopefully, been trained to think.

('There's another reason,' commented a serving officer, 'it's that guys from boarding schools are less likely to be homesick, find it far easier to settle in and cope with the discipline. Some of the kids who've never spent that long a time away from home do find it very hard, and take so long to adjust that they never really catch up.')

But the phrase to note is 'earlier-developed'. Ideally, all Marines will show integrity and responsibility. Young officers (YOs) are expected to show them earlier, and to a greater extent. Nonetheless, a typical YO

18

batch will provide a good cross section of society. Regional accents abound – and there is not that much pressure on the YOs to lose them, then or later. 'God help us if we ever become a fashionable corps,' muttered an officer, 'and forget our role as Commandos.'

Similarly, other ranks are no longer recruited exclusively from the working classes – if, indeed they ever were. There are fewer middle- or upper-class backgrounds than one would find in a YO batch, perhaps . . . but more than a sprinkling of men whose backgrounds would have destined them for the officers' mess in earlier days. Men who would probably have been accepted for officer training in the Army or Air Force. Even men who tried and failed for officer training in the Royal Marines, but decided to join the Corps anyway. For first one is a Marine, second one is an officer or other rank – a lesson that will be repeated again and again during training.

A special flair

If this suggests that Royal Marines officers are merely well-mannered thugs, it's totally wide of the mark – however much many an army officer would agree. Royal Marines officers are trained to be well-mannered, hard and extremely professional. They should also possess one other quality, which has to be apparent from the beginning: a quality that is difficult to define, but is variously called flair or personality – the ability, often bloody-minded ability, to dominate a situation. And although it's been said that officers who show too much flair find it difficult to make it to the higher echelons of command, since the job then becomes as much political as military and one should not cut too much of a dash, it is true that officers with flair will command the greatest respect and affection from their men – assuming that it's allied with both professionalism and integrity.

There's a story that's passed into Corps folklore that, perhaps, exemplifies the type of officer whom the men will respect, whatever his superiors may think of him. A Royal Marines officer had been sent on a particular course, which meant living in an army mess. Coming down to breakfast one day, he found the dining room deserted save for a Guards officer, sitting at the table and wearing his cap peak over his eyes in true Guards manner. Grunting a greeting, the Royal Marine sat down, and looked around him for a moment before asking the Guardee to pass the sugar. Absolutely no response. Not even an indication that the Marine was in the room. Again, the Marine asked for the sugar. Again, no response. He asked for a third time, and finally the Guardee condescended to speak:

'When a Guards officer wears his hat to breakfast, it is an indication that he does not wish to speak to, or be spoken to by, anyone. It is a tradition of the regiment.'

The Marine thought about it for a few moments, then climbed on to the table, walked over to the Guardee and stood in his cereal.

'When a Royal Marines officer puts his boots in your cornflakes, it means pass the bloody sugar!'

Now that probably wasn't very polite. It may even have been a tad disrespectful. But it does indicate the bloody-mindedness with flair that marks a good young officer – not to mention the aggression.

2/NODS AND YO-YOs

For the would-be Royal Marine, life begins at Lympstone. And occasionally ends there, for Lympstone proves whether or not he's capable of becoming a Royal Marine. Whether he can, one day, look forward to wearing a Green Beret, or whether his memories will always contain a 'what if' or 'might have been'

Men who have been accepted as potential Royal Marines go to the Commando Training Centre, Royal Marines, at Lympstone, South Devon, for a Potential Officer's Course (POC) or Potential Recruit's Course (PRC). There are those serving Royal Marines who claim that their PRC or POC was the hardest part of the entire thing – that it came as a total shock to the system, an experience never to be forgotten.

For those attending the PRC in particular, it's often the first time they've been away from home, isolated from the comfort of family and friends. It's the first time, possibly for all men attending a PRC or POC that they've really had to push themselves, where they've been faced with that stark fact that to choose the easy option and slow down a little means that the candidate fails. And when you think about it, failing the POC or PRC is almost worse than failing Royal Marine training itself. It means that you weren't even good enough to be considered in the first place. This brings a type of mental pressure that very few, if any, candidates would have experienced before, not even those from university, for the pressure is applied in the form of extremely competent-looking Royal Marines who challenge candidates every step of the way. Not only their abilities but their characters are being tested.

Potential Officer's Course
Not so long ago, thirty bright hopeful faces graced the breakfast table in the Lympstone Officers' Mess – the latest POC, ages ranging from seventeen to twenty-three. While one or two had simply gone along for the ride, not really caring if they passed or failed, the majority desperately wanted to be officers in the Royal Marines. That particular Monday morning dawned bright and sunny. The kids felt ready to tackle anything. The feeling didn't last.

Their first trip was to the gym where they were given – and had to pass – the USMC fitness test: eighty-five sit-ups within two minutes; sixty press-ups in as long as it took – but it better not take too long; forty squat jumps in one minute; eighteen pull-ups in as long as it took (but it better . . .); a three-hundred-metre sprint in five by sixty-metre legs, within forty-one seconds. At the end of all that, four candidates dropped out.

Next, down to the Lower Field to spend an hour or so climbing ropes. Followed by a one-hundred-and-fifty-metre fireman's carry. In the afternoon, they were taken to the Assault Course and shown how to get over the various obstacles. They were then split into teams, each team having to get themselves and a telegraph pole around the course in under twelve minutes.

The next morning they were taken to the Tarzan Course and individually tested for vertigo. After that came a fun-packed hour or so swinging (and occasionally falling) from the ropes that make up the Tarzan Course. And then they each had to give a three-minute lecture to the rest of the course. Then they were bussed up to Woodbury Common to be taken around the Endurance Course. In the afternoon came a discussion exercise, during which they were judged for fluency, intelligence, logic and the ability to dominate an audience.

By Wednesday morning only nineteen out of the original thirty were left. These were taken to the swimming pool where they had to jump in from the three-metre board, wearing full battle kit, and swim sixty metres. After that, back to the Mess to change and get their results.

Out of the original thirty only ten had passed. The rest had either quit, been told not to bother, or advised to try again when they were fitter or more mature. One of the candidates had asked an instructor what one had to do to pass. 'Show one-hundred-per-cent commitment,' came the answer, with the added proviso that it would need one-hundred-and-twenty-per-cent commitment to actually complete officer training. Whether they were capable of giving that extra commitment was later assessed at the Admiralty Interview Board.

All potential officers in the Royal Navy have to undergo an Admiralty Interview Board. The Royal Navy is the parent service of the Royal Marines. *Ergo*, potential Royal Marine officers have to attend the Admiralty Interview Board. This is where the going really gets tough. (Potential Royal Marine officers, incidentally, are not tested in quite the same way as are potential navy officers, the differences relating to ultimate job function.)

The AIB takes place at HMS *Sultan* in Gosport, Hampshire. It's composed of a rear admiral, a Royal Marines colonel or half colonel, a personnel selection officer – usually a lieutenant commander or a WRNS officer, a Royal Marines captain or major, another Royal Navy officer and a civilian headmaster, not necessarily from an independent school. Lurking somewhere in the background is also a psychologist; he does not sit on the board as such and only presents his findings on a particular candidate when the board has more or less made up its mind – his opinion being vital in borderline cases.

An AIB lasts for just under two days. It's the time when the candidates' characters and motivations are probed to see if they do have the ability and the will to give that one-hundred-and-twenty-per-cent commitment.

Candidates must show a detailed knowledge about Royal Navy history (slightly unfair, that one, but the Admiralty will have its pound of Royal Marine flesh); Royal Marine history; and Royal Marine organization and

Previous pages. Above: A timed crawl over sharp stones teaches how to endure, how to be comfortable with your rifle in unpleasant conditions. Below: Discovering the 'cold face of discipline' – drill on the square

tactics. Candidates are also probed as to why they want to be officers in the Royal Marines. And the standard reply that 'I-want-to-be-a-leader-of-men-and-serve-my-country-Sir' only ever elicits the next question: 'Why?' Since there are no pat reasons for wanting to be an officer in the Marines, there can be no pat answers.

And if the candidates breathe a sigh of relief, ever, that their next interviewer is going to be a charming and doubtless sympathetic Wren, they can forget it. 'Who would have thought,' moaned a young man who failed, 'that such a good-looking, nice woman could be so bloody hard?' Sexual equality starts at the AIB; the Wren officer in question had given that unfortunate and three others a scenario; a shipwrecked party on some bleak, inhospitable coastline, and how could they be saved? And as the candidates stammered their way from one disaster to another, the Wren pointed out their mistakes the moment they made them. Forcibly and with mounting impatience. Never had they felt so pressured – and from such an unlikely source. When the moment came that the Wren informed them that they had managed to kill off the last survivor, their sense of failure was lightened by an overwhelming relief that the ordeal was over.

Ankle and sometimes knee-deep, thick clinging black mud – and no way anyone avoids getting covered! Lympstone's infamous Mud Run is used as a mild reminder to YOs and recruits that they're there on serious business

It's pressure like this that helps to reveal the candidates in their true colours; which possibly explains why one candidate, when asked what he'd spent the last year doing as preparation for a career in the Royal Marines, answered that he'd spent it working in an abbatoir. There was another candidate who'd asked about the form of the medical exam he was due to take later. When told it would be a fairly simple affair, probably not involving more than unbuttoning his shirt, he breathed a sigh of relief, and admitted that he'd been worried in case he'd have to wear clean underpants, but as he didn't have to strip, there was no need. Needless to say, neither candidate passed, other than into the Corps folklore of the ones that got away.

In fact, of the ten original candidates who'd passed their POC, only three passed the AIB (although one was told definitely to try again the following year when he would have every chance of being successful). But even assuming four passes, possibly no more than two will make it through training. Two out of thirty. Perhaps it's the very difficulty of becoming a Royal Marine officer that makes the prospect so appealing.

Potential Recruit's Course

Potential recruits are not allowed to mix with recruits in training. Aside from the fact that the recruits in training are too busy to talk to them, they are already in another world. The three days of the PRC are going to be strange enough as it is without adding to it. Besides, recruits in training invariably spend a good deal of their time talking about leaving as soon as they can. Mostly it's a way of letting off steam, but the effect on would-be Marines could be upsetting, and they (the Corps) lose enough as it is.

When potential recruits first arrive at Lympstone – say, on a Sunday afternoon – they draw the kit they'll be using, are given a short brief about the programme, are taught elementary marching (they will not be allowed to shamble around the camp), and are taken to the induction block where they'll be staying. The lights are turned out just after 2200.

The following morning begins with a room inspection. Then comes a visit to the gym, where each man has to do as many squat jumps, sit-ups and straddle jumps as he can in one minute respectively. This tests them for physical ability, potential and mental approach – commonly known as guts.

Then comes a series of lectures about the various Technical Qualifications and Specialist Qualifications open to a Royal Marine (TQs and SQs) and how much they'll be paid. This is followed by a visit from the one recruit they do get to meet – the King's Squad Diamond. The King's Squad is the senior recruit troop in training, and the Diamond (or Diamonds, there can be more than one) is the recruit (or recruits) most likely to win the King's Badge, even though it's not always presented. Probably, the Diamond is more of an unofficial recruit NCO. It's unlikely a Diamond will tell them how perfectly bloody the whole thing is and that they should leave for home immediately. A Diamond is a very motivated man – his job is really to say yes, the training is tough, but there is light at the end of the tunnel. And if he hasn't just come back from a ten-day exercise on Dartmoor, he'll probably look as if he means it.

The following day begins with another room inspection, followed by a

First time on the Death Slide, and you may well scream all the way down. But eventually it may become fun – as long as you remember to hit the ground running because ahead lies the rest of the Tarzan Course. And that's no fun at all

1.5 mile run, to be completed in less than 11.5 minutes, followed by breakfast, and a series of character and ability interviews. Then comes a visit to the weapons museum, with a brief description of the weapons the Royal Marines use, and why, followed by a visit to the Assault Course. Here they're tested for vertigo, given a two-hundred-metre fireman's carry to do in less than ninety seconds, interviewed individually by the instructors and briefed on the following day's log race.

On the final day, after room inspection, they're taken to the Assault Course, and split into teams, and each team is presented with the inevitable telegraph pole which has to be taken around the Assault Course as quickly as possible. Unlike the POC, there's no set time – deliberately, because the instructors want to see how much pressure the recruits can apply to themselves. Log race over, stores are cleaned and returned and the potential recruits assemble to hear their fate.

For those who've failed, it can be a deeply traumatic experience. It's not unknown for a potential recruit to break down in tears when he's told by

Commando Tests – timed run over the Endurance Course, followed by regains over the tank.
Above: That loose rifle will smack him on his head when he swings off the rope. Right above: Yet another failed regain, and (right below) getting out of the tank is harder than falling in. Far right: And oh how it hurts! Close to total exhaustion, he still has to fire his rifle on the short range and hit the target

the Warrant Officer in charge that he's not been accepted, such as the young man who'd even been a member of the Royal Marines Reserve. When he'd left home to go on his PRC, so sure was he of passing that he'd told all his family and friends that the next time they saw him – some six months later – he'd be wearing the Green Beret of the fully fledged Royal Marine Commando. All he'd ever wanted to do was to join the Royal Marines. And here the door was being slammed firmly in his face, without even the comfort of being asked to try again in six months. He was merely told that it was his right to try again in a year's time – but really, wouldn't he be happier in one of the other services? For the rules are very strict. The instructors will not pass a man unless they are positive that he's capable of staying the course. Not that he's guaranteed to pass the course, merely that he's got the potential. Otherwise, it's not fair to the man, his fellow recruits, his instructors and even the Corps itself.

It's not enough that you want to do a thing so badly you've been unable to think of anything else, of any other career. This is the first harsh lesson taught by the Royal Marines – wanting is not enough, wanting does not entitle you to try. Only your own ability and real commitment can do that . . . plus the pragmatic consideration that even if you do manage to pass that course, will you be of any use to the Corps?

A team of three tackle the Water Tunnel, taking it in turn to push and pull each other through. But there's always a few seconds in the middle of the tunnel when you're on your own, wondering if you'll make it

A question of commitment

Officers train at Lympstone for a total of forty-seven weeks, recruits for thirty. Including holidays, that makes a year for officers and six months for recruits. The difference between the two courses is that a YO does have to learn far more – when he leaves Lympstone, although he's still on probation for another year, he's expected to be able to begin to command a troop (equivalent to an army platoon, theoretically numbering thirty or so men), whereas a young Marine leaving Lympstone is only expected to be able to take his *place* in a troop. Both will still be faced with a deal of learning, but the responsibilities of a 'sprog' officer in the Corps are that much greater – he's trained to take command from the beginning, whereas in the army he may often spend the first year or so as another officer's second in command. But of the two, the army system is probably preferable since it gives the officer more time to grow into the job – and possibly more practical experience.

The sheer intensity and professionalism of the training at Lympstone comes as a total shock to YO and recruit alike. Tough as the POC, AIB and PRC were, they were no indication of what training will really be like. A subtle change has come over the instructors, too. Before, they appeared to be encouraging them to pass. Now, they appear to be challenging them to fail – sometimes even encouraging them to fail. Most YOs and recruits start out by making up a calendar to chart their progress week by week, month by month. The calendar is soon ignored. It is as much as they can do to get by on a day-to-day basis – sometimes, from morning to afternoon – without even thinking what next week or next month will bring. Reasons for joining are soon forgotten, appear trivial when men are living for days on end in a narrow trench – a narrow, flooded trench with the temperature below freezing. Or when they're speed marching nine miles with equipment weighing up to thirty pounds on their backs (just a foretaste of what life will be like in a unit). It is not why they joined that's important. It's why they stay. And that depends on how truly committed they were (for a sense of commitment often outlasts more logical reasons) and how determined they are not to be beaten. It becomes a very personal battle: the man (or rather the YO batch or recruit troop, because no man can succeed on his own) against the course itself. Certainly loyalty to one's fellow YOs or recruits will become one of the biggest reasons for not quitting.

This is as it should be, for as author James Jones noted in *The Thin Red Line*, men do not, in battle, normally commit acts of bravery and endurance out of loyalty to an abstract ideal. They do so out of loyalty to each other, which makes far more sense, because they're less likely to get each other killed, or to expect someone else to die for their own beliefs.

The instructors demand that YOs and recruits grow up very quickly. All the instructors have served with one or other of the commandos. All will have seen action in Northern Ireland or the Falklands. All make it very plain that playtime is over and this is for real. For although it is extremely difficult to simulate battlefield conditions during training – far too expensive and resulting in an unacceptable casualty rate (and God knows it's high enough to begin with) – you *can* simulate the mental and physical pressures of the battlefield. This is exactly what the instructors

You need strength, agility and
determination to traverse two
ropes like this, fuelled by the
knowledge that if you fall off,
you'll have to do it again . . . and
again . . . and again until you
get it right

try to do, while teaching YOs and recruits their trade. Learn how to fire
and clean your rifle. Learn how to do it when you're dog tired, at night,
living in two feet of mud and already late for the next rendezvous. Learn
how to keep yourself and your clothes clean. Learn how to do it when
there are only minutes between lectures, no matter what the programme
claims. Learn how to go around the Endurance Course in a three- or
four-man syndicate, each helping the other. Learn how to do it when one
man's injured and if you don't achieve the correct time, you'll all have to
go round again. Learn how to lead or take part in a troop attack. Learn
how to do it when you haven't slept for three days and you're suffering
from mild exposure. Learn how to live out in the wilds for a week or so.
Learn how to do it when you've fallen into a river (not a deliberate part of
the curriculum) and you, plus all your spare clothes, are soaking wet with
little prospect of drying out. Above all, perhaps, learn how to take
responsibility for your mates. Learn how to do this when there are at least
three or four of them you can't stand – and who can't stand you. A yo-yo's
(YO) or nod's (recruit) life is not an easy one.

Potential Recruit Training
If those who've passed the PRC and arrived back at Lympstone to begin
their training proper think that they can immediately become part of
recruit training proper, they're sadly mistaken. First, they have two weeks
in an induction block – time intended to bring them to the point of
beginning to be recruits. Time for the Corps to take a much closer look at
them and decide if it really does want them. Time, come to that, for the
recruits to take a closer look at the Corps and decide if they still want to
become Marines.

The two weeks are spent learning the more basic aspects of soldiering:
how to wash and iron one's own clothes and how to keep the living
accommodation clean and tidy. Let it be said that these two aspects of
recruit training are not a reflection on the standard of recruits applying to
join the Royal Marines (despite the basic academic standard required,
many boast two or more A levels, and may have joined from a successful
job in civvy street). It is more a comment on the fact that today's young
men appear to be far more spoilt than those of a decade or so ago. Spoilt
not just by their parents, but by fashions and fabrics, for example, that
appear to require very little ironing – or by the ready availability of dry
cleaners and washing machines. By the fact that trainers (sneakers) don't
need polishing – whereas military boots do, because if they're not
polished, the leather will crack and no longer be waterproof. The shine is
just an added bonus.

This is a time when the recruits begin to think like recruits, when they
realize how ill-equipped they are to last the training, when they begin to
understand that military discipline in the Royal Marines is largely a matter
of self-discipline. No instructor will continually badger a recruit to do a
certain job. He'll tell him once, and that's it. Often, he won't tell him at
all, expecting that the recruit will see the necessity of doing such-and-such
before he gets shouted out – it's called developing one's initiative.

This is a time, too, when the recruits first make their acquaintance with
the drill square. Much to their surprise, they discover that Royal Marine

Opposite, above: The new
SA80 is so accurate that
standards have had to be
revised upwards

Opposite, below: A map reading
lesson – note how the recruits
keep hold of their rifles. They
must learn to think of their rifles
as part of their own bodies

drill instructors do not scream in high falsettos – do not go in for the eyeball-to-eyeball confrontation that one finds at Quantico (USMC) or Catterick (Brigade of Guards). Commands are audible, but shouted only if the troop is some distance away. And a rebuke – the recruits soon discover – is all the more effective if it's delivered in a coldly contemptuous tone, almost conversationally, rather than screamed into one's ear from a distance of two inches. At the end of the two weeks the recruits can decide if they want to stay or not. The Corps can decide if it wants to keep them or not – although the Corps can decide to dispense with a man's services whenever it wants to. Between twenty and forty per cent will leave at this point. Some leave because they've become intensely homesick, others because they've realized that there are easier ways of impressing a girlfriend.

Recently, one recruit was 'let go' when it was discovered that he didn't know how to wash himself – although he was eighteen, his mother had always supervised bath time. Most instructors – particularly the drill instructors who also act as surrogate parents to the recruits – will go to considerable lengths to help the lads adapt to the rigours and confines of training. But bathing one by hand is stretching this a little too far.

The two weeks up, the recruits now move out of the induction block into proper recruit accommodation. Not that it's all that different, more a sign that they're considered fit to mix with more senior recruits.

And now the pressure really begins. They discover that their instructors actually appear to be encouraging them to leave (which they can do, but not until their twelfth week). 'Go on, make my day and wrap [quit]' is an an oft-heard refrain – which usually has the desired effect of making the recruits want to stay and tough it out, even if it's only to prove the instructor wrong.

'Believe me,' said an instructor, 'if we were too kind and understanding in the beginning, we'd lose far more than we do.' The point is that no one is going to drag a recruit through training. It's something that he must do, can only do, for himself.

By the same token, the recruits are not broken down and then reassembled in the Corps image – as tends to happen in the USMC or the French Foreign Legion. Brainwashing is out, if for no other reason than that brainwashing creates men with little initiative – and is ineffectual anyway at moments of stress, leading to a breakdown in battlefield discipline. Rather, the corps encourages the recruits (and YOs) to grow in those directions that will help them to become Marines, to grow both physically and psychologically, to become elite soldiers in body and mind.

But recruits are never that much aware of the mental changes they're going through. Only when they look back at the end of it all and compare their characters then with the type of men they are now, do they realize that they have undergone a sea change from boy to Marine.

A good deal has been reported about 'beasting' at Lympstone – the unmerciful bullying of recruits by savage and sadistic instructors. Undoubtedly, it does happen occasionally. In a Corps numbering some seven thousand men, there'll always be at least one bad apple. And Sod's Law (the Corps version of Murphy's Law) states that not only *will* something always go wrong, but that it'll go wrong in a manner calculated

to produce the worst publicity for the Royal Marines. Nonetheless, true cases of beasting are mercifully rare and are dealt with severely. What does often happen is that neither recruit nor parent (nor the parent's local Member of Parliament who inevitably becomes involved) realizes that recruits are not being trained to look good in their Green Berets; not to look good on guard outside Buckingham Palace; not even to exercise interminably with 42 and 45 Commando in Norway. A recruit is trained to fight and survive on the battlefield, as a commando, as a Royal Marine. Again, it's a question of simulating the mental and physical pressures that occur in war. But at the same time, the instructors are not only being cruel to be kind. They are attempting to turn out Marines who can do their job – and if being able to do that job means the ability to eat a dead rat and fire a rifle before the other guy, that's what they'll teach.

Not, one hastens to add, that recruits at Lympstone are ever taught to eat dead rats – dead rabbits that they've killed themselves, yes. Dead rats, no. But they are taught to develop the ability to do whatever they must to get the job done. Again, not in terms of savagery in war, but in terms of being able to drive themselves to the very limit and beyond. And it is an inescapable fact that no one ever knows what they're truly capable of until they're forced to find out.

The longest days

There's a week-by-week breakdown of recruit training on page 188. For now, let's take a look at a 'day-in-the-life-of' a recruit in, say, the tenth week of training, nearly half way through the course. One thing's for sure, this recruit wouldn't stand out in a crowd of other recruits for they all tend to look alike. It's not their comparative youth. Nor their short hair. Nor the fact that they all wear identical clothes. It's the fact that all recruits have the same deadpan expressions. In the early stages of training the only emotions they appear to show are dismay (when something's gone wrong, and it always does) or relief (when something's gone wrong but the instructors haven't noticed. Yet). A deadpan face is the natural camouflage of the recruit, reflecting a desire to go unnoticed from one embuggerance to another.

Even asleep, recruits all look alike – which is how we first meet this particular man, lying in his bed at 0330. But not for long, as the door is flung open and he plus the rest of the troop are told by an instructor to get dressed (in PT kit) and get outside.

By now the recruit has learnt not to ask too many questions, but to accept as cheerfully as possible everything that comes his way. There is a reason, he's sure, for shaking him and his mates out of bed at an ungodly hour – and that reason is bound to be Something They've Done (or Not Done). Sometimes, it's better not to ask.

It's cold outside and the troop stands shivering for a while before being marched off towards the water tank. This is an open-air tank measuring some forty feet across. Its metal sides are about eight feet tall, the water inside is five feet deep. Ropes are strung some eight feet above the surface – single ropes, reasonably taut but not so taut that they won't swing and sway when someone is crawling across them. Here the recruit troop is told to practise regains for the next half hour. A regain is the method by which having crawled half way across the tank on top of the rope, you stop, let yourself down so you're hanging by your hands, and then try to swing back on top of the rope again to carry on crawling. It is very difficult at the best of times; it requires strength, and agility and timing. At nearly four in the morning, it's well nigh impossible. Within a few minutes all the recruits are wet.

At that point one of the instructors gently reminds them that the previous day's weapon inspection had been bad in the extreme. Dirty barrels, dirty moving parts, mud-encrusted magazines – over half the troop had had something wrong with their rifles – and this after being warned that an inspection was due. In itself that had been a mark of favour, since recruits are not normally warned but are expected to keep their rifles spotless at all times. As the instructor points out, it's unlikely that so many of them will fail an inspection ever again. Somehow the recruits feel that he's telling the truth.

That lesson over, it's back to the barracks for as much sleep as they can get before reveille at 0600.

Our recruit gets up, grabs a quick shower, shaves, makes his bed and does his share of the barrackroom chores. He tries to be as quick as he can, because breakfast is at 0630 and he has to draw his rifle from the armoury before 0700. If he's lucky he'll have about twenty-five minutes to check his rifle for cleanliness – very important after the earlier event – help to give the room a once-over, get his kit ready for the day and get dressed for first parade at 0800. This lasts for the best part of an hour and is followed by three-quarters of an hour's drill.

Between 0845 and 0940 he has a map-reading lecture. The instructor continually questions the class to make sure that they understand and are not simply pretending to do so. Map reading over, the recruit has ten minutes to get ready for the next lecture, on platoon or troop tactics, to be held on the Lower Field. Platoon or troop tactics are over by 1035. According to the timetable he then has a ten-minute stand easy (tea break). But the next lecture is PT in the gymnasium, for which he has to get changed. Together with his troop he doubles back to the accommodation block, gets changed, and doubles over to the gym. No stand easy – some recruits claim that they never had a stand easy throughout their training, were convinced it was a figment of someone's imagination.

PT finishes at 1140 and he has ten minutes to get showered, get changed again and be with his rifle at the next venue for weapon training. Lunch is between 1235 and 1335. He spends most of this time making sure he's ready for the afternoon. AT 1335 – on the dot – he's on the 25-metre range for live firing, which ends at 1440. He then has the inevitable ten minutes to get back to his barrackroom, stow his rifle in his locker, make sure the locker's locked and muster outside where a three-ton truck is waiting to take the troop to Woodbury Common for a map-reading exercise, when he'll be tested on the morning's lecture. Woodbury Common is the most relaxed part of the day so far. He even has time to notice another recruit troop, two months senior to his own, who are on exercise up there. He notices, somewhat enviously, that those recruits appear to be far more in command of the situation – and that their instructors appear to treat them as being at least semi-human. Map reading finishes at 1630 and, since the truck has vanished, the troop must run the four miles back to the camp. His rifle and any other stores must be cleaned and returned by 1730. Supper is at 1745. He wolfs down his food, in a hurry to get some time to himself before official lights out at 2230. In reality, he's still up and the lights are still blazing at 2230 since he has to help a mate with the other man's ironing – a favour which will be returned the next day.

And as he does finally fall asleep, he wonders – not for the first time – why on earth he wanted to join the Royal Marines. And shouldn't he opt out in week twelve as is his right? For if he doesn't do so then, short of a medical discharge – or being simply declared unsuitable by the Corps – he's theirs for the next four years. And then he may remember the other recruits he saw on Woodbury Common, and how they appeared to be coping so well, and he'll probably promise himself to give it one last go before calling home with the news that he couldn't hack it after all.

Every recruit wants to leave at some time or other during training. The course wouldn't be hard enough if he didn't. And if the above 'day-in-the-life-of' appears to be lacking in commando skills, and mainly concentrates on the type of training one could expect in any military unit, there's a reason. You cannot teach a man all those arcane disciplines that help to make him an elite soldier unless you get the basics right. Before he's a Commando he must be a very good soldier indeed. He must also grow from adolescent to mature man in a far shorter time than nature or society usually allows.

One of our sheep is missing

In fact, recruits are introduced to those commando skills quite early on in their training – but on exercise, in the field where it counts. Their first taste of being a Commando comes in week twelve, on an exercise called either Omega Man or Hunter's Moon – both rather emotive names which conjure up much skulduggery and creeping about at night. But while they appear, at face value, to be the stuff of *Boy's Own* books and war comics, the reality is – as always – very different.

In principle the exercise is a simple one. The recruits are taken to a fairly deserted part of the moors (usually Exmoor), given an area to live in and told to get on with it.

It begins with drawing stores. Each recruit can take a set of denims; a pair of overalls (ovies), a waterproof jacket (made of nylon so that sweat vapour condenses inside and makes one's clothes damp); two pairs of socks, a shirt, underwear, a pullover if it's really cold (woolly pully); a pair of boots and a sleeping bag. (The sleeping bag is a comparatively recent innovation. Not so very long ago, the recruits were allowed to take only a single blanket.)

The recruits are also issued with a survival kit – fish hooks, nylon line, waterproof matches etc., mainly useful for the psychological comfort it brings. Additionally the troop will take radios, maps, compasses, protractors – and also load on to the three-ton truck all the stores that the instructors will take with them – a somewhat poignant moment as they lift up stoves and camp beds and tents and food. For the meal they have before leaving will be the last real meal for at least two days.

The troop is then trucked to Exmoor, disembarked in a lonely spot and

Exercise Hunter's Moon, and a recruit proudly shows the remains of his lunch. Never mind that the fish was a scant three inches long – he caught it himself. Besides, it helped flavour the nettle soup

Exercise Hunter's Moon and time to learn from their own mistakes – these recruits should've put the metal sheeting on the roof first, then the plastic, everything finished with mud, grass and leaves for camouflage and insulation

searched for any contraband items like chocolate bars, cigarettes or even money – particularly money, since one troop managed to smuggle out quite a considerable sum and used it to pay a local farmer's wife to cook for them.

'Great initiative, lads,' one of the instructors is reputed to have said, 'Now let's see you yomp [trek] back to camp.'

The search over, two instructors lead them across the moor for some twelve miles, at night, to the area where they're to set up camp. This tends to be in a well-wooded valley that runs quite precipitously down to a river or stream. Here the recruits will make their brushwood 'bivvies', using whatever materials they can find in that one area. But there's never any time – or enough light – to make a bivvie on the first night. Instead, the recruits grab whatever branches they can find, make some sort of rudimentary shelter, and huddle together inside. If nothing else, this does wonders in dispelling any inhibitions they may have about cuddling up to each other for warmth.

The next day, and depending on the weather conditions, they may be given one tarpaulin (a small tarpaulin) between four of them. Or if they've been allowed to take ponchos (and this decision is left up to each individual training team) they can tie them together to make a single sheet. With that as a basic floor covering – and sometimes as any sort of covering, if it's too warm for sleeping bags – they begin to make their bivvies. The training team will offer some advice, but mostly they watch to see which recruit is coping well, which recruit has remembered the lecture on the subject or is showing some initiative – and which recruits are either content to follow someone else's lead, or are beginning to sink into damp apathy (damp because it's nearly always raining). Most importantly, the instructors are watching for the recruits who appear to be determined to enjoy the experience, who can still keep their sense of humour even as it dawns on them that this is not going to be the fun time that they'd imagined. For it's one thing to be told that you're going to have to live off the land, another to be faced with the difficulty of doing so – and subsequently, of not eating at all. (It's doubly hard when the smell of cooking from the instructors' tent often wafts across in your direction . . . .)

On one survival exercise in 1986 the weather conditions were so bad that two recruits went down with exposure on the first night and the training team had quickly to pitch a marquee to shelter the rest of the troops from freezing rain and gale-force winds. Both recruits were taken to hospital that same night – and taken back out to the exercise the following morning.

'It was really rather pitiful,' remembered an instructor who'd fetched them from hospital, 'the way one of them lay there, staring up at me, his little eyes pleading not to be taken from his nice warm bed. But the doc had passed him fit (a civilian doctor) and so back out he had to go. Nurses thought I was some sort of monster. The nod knew I was. But the main thing wrong with him was simply lack of guts. If you think you can't make it, if you don't want to dig out and try and make it, you won't – you'll go down, no question.'

Recruits in the field on a survival exercise are meant to be tactical most of the time, meaning that they must assume that an enemy may attack at any moment. They are not, to be truthful, as tactical as they will be in some other exercises – when they'll spend many hours, even days, wearing NBC suits (anti nuclear, bacteriological and chemical warfare protection clothing), but they can expect the occasional thunderflash thrown in their direction, invariably when they're just getting off to sleep. Nor are they necessarily told what the exercise programme is going to be. Again, the training staff are looking for those recruits who either react well or badly when one surprise after another is thrown at them.

The same troop who suffered so badly on their first night experienced just such a surprise two nights later. They were still living in the marquee. Conditions were simply too bad to allow them out on the moor, even in the comparative safety of a wooded one-in-four slope. But as the marquee was a mere few yards away from the instructors' own tent complex, meaning that the recruits were continuously aware how warm and dry – not to mention well fed – the instructors were, any scant extra comfort was offset by a certain mental torment. The recruits had been allowed to settle down for the night, when they were suddenly woken up. They were told that a night navigation exercise (night navex) had been planned; that they were to get up, get into their wet clothes (leaving their dry ones for when they returned) and muster outside as soon as possible. There they were issued

Half way through the final exercise and a wise recruit checks his feet before that night's twenty-mile yomp

38

with radios, maps and one emergency bergen (rucksack) per four-man team. The route was explained to them – eight miles, passing through four checkpoints across the highest part of Exmoor – and they were marched to the starting line and sent off at staggered intervals. But not before one of the teams had reported to the training sergeant that one of their number – the recruit who'd gone down with exposure and hadn't wanted to leave his hospital bed – had become totally withdrawn, wouldn't say a word except to complain about the cold, and they really didn't want the responsibility of taking him up on to the moor. The sergeant sent for the recruit and asked him if he was fit enough to take part in the night navex. The recruit hummed and hawed for some time before allowing that he didn't really think so – but that he wanted to do it in case he was back-trooped.

(A recruit who misses part of the training, or appears to be physically incapable of doing it, or is injured, may be back-trooped, i.e. spend some time in a remedial troop before joining a totally new one. Recruits hate to be back-trooped because it means making new friends. It also means spending that much longer at Lympstone.)

In reality, this particular recruit had guessed that failure to complete the exercise would probably mean being discharged from the Corps – as turned out to be the case. The training team had had their eye on him for some time, feeling that probably he should never have been accepted as a recruit in the first place.

And so, minus one recently hospitalized recruit, thankful to be now out of it and already looking forward to the day when he would leave Lympstone altogether, the team set off.

For all that it's supposed to be so beautiful, Exmoor is a wicked place. Somehow its hills seem steeper than those on Dartmoor. Being so close to the Bristol Channel and thus the Atlantic, Exmoor catches the full force of those gales that sweep in from the sea. The fact that more of it is cultivated than Dartmoor works against the night walker too: more barbed-wire fences – often just a single strand, invisible in the darkness – to rip and tear. The temperature was close to freezing – cold enough to make the recruits want to run all the way. As it was, they managed to trot a good deal of it. They also discovered, by good map reading, that if they missed out the one checkpoint that was unmanned, so saving about two miles, it would still be possible to approach the next checkpoint from the correct direction. As against that, they *had* been told to go to each checkpoint, and if they were caught they knew they'd have to go round again. In the end, the two miles that could be saved won the day and the team managed to complete the night navex without being found out.

And if to the casual observer it seemed that they spent so much time in checking the new route they had to follow – so much time and energy in making sure they approached the manned checkpoint from the right direction, that they might just as well have done the thing properly – that wasn't the point. It was that, by using the skills the instructors had taught them, they had managed to outsmart the instructors themselves. Any time a recruit can get one over on his instructors, he's a happy man.

This attitude came to a head a few years ago. It all started when the recruit training wing received a phone call from a local Exmoor farmer. He was missing two sheep, couldn't even find the bodies, and since a recruit

Above and below: Abseiling and rope work at Foggin Tor, Dartmoor. Using the 'roller haulage' technique, a recruit is pulled up the cliff face

Opposite: The nerve-wracking 'run down' requires total faith in the instructor controlling the man's rate of descent

troop had been in his area a month or so before he wondered if they'd seen or heard anything suspicious – like a wild dog, or even strangers with a van.

The message was passed to the training team who'd taken the troop into the area. No, there'd been nothing suspicious, though the troop in question had looked far happier and well fed than they should have done. The instructors had remarked on it at the time, and merely concluded that for once they had a bunch of exceptionally well-switched-on men, and left it at that. But then the instructors remembered that amongst the troop was a man who had been a butcher in civilian life . . . surely he, *they* couldn't have? But they had. Two sheep had been captured, stunned, expertly slaughtered, butchered, cooked and devoured. The troop admitted their guilt by the fact that when they were told they would have to pay for the animals, they did so without question. Smugly, and without question. 'You know,' an officer said, 'you could almost be proud of them – to do that under the very noses of the training team and not get caught. Except of course that one is so terribly shocked by the whole thing. . . .'

Since that day, recruits have been kept well away from sheep. Now, the only meat they have to eat on their survival exercise is the rabbits which are given to them at some stage – given to them live, and which they then have to kill, skin, and clean before eating. It is the first time that most recruits have ever killed anything in their lives.

'Killing itself isn't the point of the exercise,' explained an instructor, 'or it better not be. God help any recruit who we think actually enjoys it. See, it's not that we're starting them off on killing rabbits and graduating them on to killing enemy soldiers, maybe by way of a few politicians. What it is, it's a hard lesson in self-sufficiency. And they learn that no matter how squeamish you may think you are, there comes a time when you're so cold, tired and hungry that your scruples vanish. Not that we'll make a guy kill a rabbit if he honestly can't bring himself to do so – but that's not for his sake, it's for the rabbit's. A nervous guy will botch it, and that'll make the animal suffer.'

The recruits are told that if they don't manage to kill their rabbit quickly and cleanly, an instructor *will* make them suffer for it. This produces a slight nervousness – often manifesting itself in a certain black humour. It is not uncommon to see a line of recruits, each holding a rabbit and waiting their turn at the killing block, suddenly launch into a chorus of 'Bright Eyes' from *Watership Down*. Not quite what Art Garfunkel had in mind.

Lessons learned

What do they learn from exercises like these? For many of them, city born and bred, it's learning to get closer, almost to merge with nature in the wild. For all, it's a time when they discover that they can manage to survive even though the only hot drink they've had in three days is nettle tea. That in itself brings a tremendous sense of accomplishment. But then, all of recruit training is designed to do just that – to build up their self-esteem by giving them a succession of harder and harder tasks. In the process they graduate from being boys to becoming a certain kind of man – not necessarily the kind of man today's society feels totally at home with, but the kind of man society needs to defend it.

Officer Training

A brief glance at the YO training curriculum (see below) shows the emphasis laid on military skills. For the Royal Marine YO is, after all, trained to lead a troop numbering some thirty men – in theory. In practice, detachments, courses, leave and undermanning may result in a troop considerably smaller. If nothing else, this makes him re-evaluate his tactics.

As a troop commander, the YO will be totally responsible for the welfare and administration of his men. Naturally, he'll have alongside him an experienced troop sergeant – but however much the officer may lean on the sergeant in the beginning, there must come a day when he's fully capable of taking over. Otherwise he runs the possibility of failing the year's probationary period that follows the year already spent at Lympstone, and being asked to resign his commission.

That Royal Marine officers are expected to take on such early responsibility is reflected in their pay – a Royal Marines captain, for example, is paid the same as an army major. Nor is it uncommon to find a Royal Marines captain or lieutenant doing a job that would be done by an army major or captain. Against that, promotion tends to be slower in the Corps than in the army, if only because there are fewer jobs available. In terms of YO training at Lympstone, this means that the course is designed to produce young officers (sprog officers in Marine-speak) who are trained to a higher military standard at troop or platoon commander level than their equivalents from Sandhurst. And while the course of thirty-four weeks is the longest of its type in the world – and arguably the toughest, since the physical pressure is applied from Day One – it is not generally felt to be long enough. A tremendous amount of work is crammed into a relatively short space of time.

If there is a comparison with civilian life, it would probably be likening YO studying for an honours degree while also training to compete in the Pentathlon at international standard.

YOUNG OFFICER TRAINING CURRICULUM

Weeks 1–10
Personal administration (YOs have to know how to do their own washing and ironing). Drill; Physical Training; Weapon Training; Map Reading; Field Craft; First Aid; Signals; Recreational Training; Corps History; Leadership.

Weeks 11–20
Sword Drill; Basic Fitness Tests; Weapon Training; Written and Spoken Orders; Patrolling; Tactics; Military Organizations; Helicopter Drills; Current Affairs; Nuclear Bacteriological and Chemical Warfare (NBC); Military Law; Signals; Service Writing.

Weeks 21–30
PT; Soviet/Warsaw Pact Forces; Other Front-line Units; Troop Tactics; Current Affairs; Assault Engineering; Staff Duties; NBC Warfare; Signals.

Weeks 31–34 (Commando Course)
PT; Weapon Training (field firing); Climbing; Raiding Techniques.
One week of tests.

Weeks 34–45
Troop Commander Responsibilities; Weapon Training; Man Management (admin/welfare); Final Exercise and Pass-out.

Weeks 46–47
Two weeks at Poole learning about Landing Craft and the Special Boat Service.

To pass out successfully as officers, YOs must also pass every subject on the curriculum. Since over half these subjects are essentially academic, this requires a good deal of late-night study.

The pressure on YOs to 'grow up and grow into the job' is far greater than on recruits. Whereas recruits may, often are, told in some detail about their mental or psychological shortcomings and suggestions made as to how they can overcome them, YOs are generally expected to sort out those problems for themselves.

A YO asking one of his instructors how he could best improve in a certain direction is liable to be given short shrift. At the most he can expect the question: 'Well, Mr So-and-So, how do *you* think you can best improve?' In this way YOs are far more aware of the maturing process they're going through – and far more aware of the penalties of failure.

The physical horrors of YO training are worse than those facing recruits. For while the demands are very much the same, the average YO is expected to perform better than the average recruit. In fact, the most incompetent YO is expected to perform better than the average recruit. The Royal Marines do not believe that leadership is a function of class or education, but that it is a function of a man's ability to win the respect and trust of those whom he would lead – and in the very physical sense, of being able to keep up with them in the field, in battle.

YOs are trained mainly by Royal Marine sergeants with Royal Marine officers overseeing the course and taking some of the lectures. It has been suggested in the press that the sergeants take this opportunity to impress their charges with a 'Sergeants Rule, OK' philosophy. Nothing could be further from the truth. YOs leaving Lympstone will probably go to a troop whose sergeant is a personal friend of the men who've been training him. And since all senior NCOs are well aware of the importance of having officers, and the vital role a troop officer plays in war, they are unlikely to turn out meek and cringing men who will do whatever the troop sergeant tells them. To do so would be to court disaster.

Perhaps it's best at this point to try to explain what the function of an officer in the Royal Marines is (not so very different to an officer's function in the army) and how he interacts with his senior NCOs and men, particularly at troop level.

However the distinction between officers and men first came about, it is today based on several unassailable facts. First, men do need a 'figurehead', someone to inspire them, someone they can trust, particularly in times of stress.

Second, it's far easier for a man to make life-and-death decisions about other men if he's one step removed from them, if his rank carries with it the implied right to make such decisions.

Third, a man cannot be expected to make decisions continually about men under his command unless there is someone who can help him to implement them, i.e. his senior and junior NCOs (colour sergeants, sergeants and corporals).

Fourth, as a system it works extremely well. And until another one can be proved equally effective, no one is going to change it.

This means that senior NCOs act as a type of middle management. They are the link between officers and men. And while, at troop level, it would be a foolhardy officer who always makes decisions without asking his sergeant for his opinion, at the end of the day the sole responsibility is the officer's alone. Rule by committee does not work on the battlefield.

Recruits disembark the easy (dry!) way from an LCVP during their final exercise

All military rank structures are designed to work in times of war, not peace. Where the Royal Marines differ perhaps from some other units is that they expect a good officer to command by virtue of his ability and personality and not by virtue of a piece of paper saying that he's been awarded a commission by the Queen. And that his men had better obey him, or else. It is for this function that YOs are trained at Lympstone. That is why it's in their instructors' own best interests that they produce the type of officer whom they would, one day, be happy to serve with. Indeed, given the relatively small size of the Corps, it's quite possible that a YO training sergeant will at some time serve with an officer he once trained.

The situation is affected by the fact that Royal Marine senior NCOs are generally regarded (by the USMC in particular) as being the best in the world. This in itself puts an enormous pressure on YOs in training; they have a far higher standard to follow and live up to – a standard set by men who are nominally inferior in rank and status.

Sometimes this situation results in a YO effectively hero worshipping his instructors – a situation the instructors themselves try hard to discourage since the man must learn to stand on his own feet, must finish training convinced in his own mind that he's capable, in the not so distant future, of leading the very men who have been teaching him. In a similar way, a student at university may well be extremely grateful for the advice, the teaching his tutor gives him. He may respect his tutor enormously, but a certain type of student will want to better his tutor one day – out of the realization that if he's to be successful in his chosen career, that is the standard to aim for. Ambition does play a major part in a YO successfully completing training.

YOs United

Probably one of the biggest contrasts between YO and recruit training was pinpointed by the man who'd gained a Corps Commission. (There are a limited number of Corps Commissions open to trained Marines under the age of twenty-seven.)

This particular YO said that the difference was that he could ask as many questions as he liked as a YO – was encouraged to do so – whereas recruits were not given quite the same leeway. Describing himself as 'a bit of a gobby [talkative] bastard, really', he also pointed out that while recruits could often relax at night, YOs had to study: less free time, less opportunity for sleep.

In order to get through training, YOs must – like recruits – work together. Like recruits, a YO batch will turn a united front to the rest of the world. Like recruits, YOs will not suffer a man to stay if he neither fits in nor pulls his weight.

'I remember one guy in my batch,' reminisced a serving officer, 'who was got rid of by the rest of us. It just seemed obvious that he wasn't cut out for the life, never tried to mix with the other guys, kit was always shambolic, so we simply asked him again and again if he *really* wanted to be a Marine. After a month or so he wrapped [quit] and having experienced life in a troop since then, I think we were right to behave like that. No way could he have survived.'

Welcome to Salisbury Plain

It's true. Battlefields, even simulated battlefields, do possess a certain beauty at night. But the eerie green of the flares, the flash and delayed crump! of the explosive charges, felt before being heard, and the crack of their own weapons, were aesthetically wasted on the section of YOs practising live firing at night on a very wet and cold Salisbury Plain.

They had been in position for well over an hour, lying full length in the mud, the rain trickling down their backs and oozing through to their skin – not for the first time prompting the question 'What the hell am I doing here, anyway?'

What they had been doing was waiting for a sergeant instructor to appear with the remote-control radio transmitter that would activate the targets they were to shoot at – that they were to shoot at and hit. No matter how bad the weather, no matter how tired and cold they were (barely five hours' sleep in the past four days), they were expected to be at their best.

Their sergeant had finally arrived together with the assault engineer who'd spent the previous afternoon laying charges that would simulate grenade, artillery and mortar fire. The control box was produced, the button pressed and suddenly the area was illuminated by flares, followed immediately by explosion after explosion as the charges disintegrated in a shower of mud and stones. Simultaneously, targets popped up in front of the section. The section leader for the night remained calm and gave the correct fire orders – an overexcited, ragged volley would not have been permissible. And the first few rounds were disciplined, the right men shooting at the specified targets, before the order 'Fire At Will' came, allowing the YOs to pepper the targets as they liked – targets that were falling down and springing up again like so many demented jack in the boxes – and all the time the bright green of the flares, the noise of explosions and a shower of earth as a charge exploded nearby.

That phase of the exercise had been designed to accustom the YO to fire weapons, not in the comparative peace and tranquillity of the range, but in highly unpleasant surroundings. To fire and hit the target without forgetting safety drills. (To learn to be as professional as possible – for if he's not, when he's posted to a unit, both brother officers and senior NCOs – not to mention his men – will soon let him know exactly what they think of him.)

That night, the YOs had done well. Good, accurate fire. Good weapon drills. The only slight mistake occurred after the firing had stopped and the section leader had begun to lead the other YOs out of the valley. The pass he'd chosen would have taken them directly into the path of live rounds being fired by a machine gun some thirty feet further up the hillside.

'Dear me,' said the training sergeant, 'we are feeling a little confused tonight. . . . Not that way, Mr —, think of all the paperwork I'd have to do. Follow the contour line we're on until the GPMG [general purpose machine gun] is well behind us.'

It is an interesting experience to walk along the side of a valley with a machine gun firing away over your head – firing live tracer rounds that streak away into the darkness before impacting with an audible thump on the target area. Rounds that sound as if they're at least the size of chickens'

Above: Live tracer firing at night over the heads of YOs on Salisbury Plain

Right: The YOs had dug their trenches. They'd lived in them for a week. Now they had to fill them in, leaving the area much as they found it

eggs, even though you know they're only a few centimetres long. Even though you know that the machine gun is on a fixed mounting – and that's secured to a concrete block buried deep into the earth – you can't help but wonder what would happen if the mounting suddenly broke and the gun barrel depressed to fire directly at your own little group.

And when the training sergeant says conversationally, 'It was like that on Mount Harriet [in the Falklands], except then the bastards were firing down at us,' you suddenly realize how important training is – and if you're a YO, how lucky you are to have as a training sergeant a man who won the Military Medal for his actions during the Falklands War.

Safely away from the SF (SF = Sustained Fire = machine gun), the section had made their way out of the valley to where they could be inspected.

It is a crime, punishable by Court Martial, for any soldier of any rank to have any unauthorized ammunition in his possession, particularly during an exercise, when live rounds can easily become mixed up with blank rounds. The YOs had given all their live ammo to the training team before lining up to be searched.

'I have no live rounds in my possession, Sergeant': a time-honoured, legal statement followed by a thorough search of each YO's webbing pouches and his combat suit pockets. But one YO was discovered to have three live rounds still in his possession, and the dressing down he received was shattering.

'You were told. You were warned. You know the dangers. You're supposed to be a man, a leader. So for God's sake behave like one – get over there, put the live rounds with the rest of the spares. There's no excuse. If you can't learn to look after yourself and obey orders, how the hell do you think you'll be able to lead a troop and look after the men under your command?'

The rebuke was doubly devastating because it was delivered by a man the YO both liked and respected. But that YO will never forget his range safety again, nor will any of the other YOs in the section.

Finally, the section made its way back to the trenches they had been living in for the past week – a week in which they'd been bombarded by thunderflashes, subjected to simulated gas attacks and overrun by tanks.

Tank trap

Admittedly, there had been a slight mistake during the tank attack.

The entire YO batch had joined up with young army officers who were on a command course at nearby Warminster. The difference was, as one of the Marine YOs ruefully commented, the army officers were allowed to go back to a nice, warm officers' mess at night whereas the Marines had naught for comfort but a three-foot by fifteen-foot trench – admittedly roofed over in parts, but still narrow, wet and uncomfortable.

On the afternoon before the live firing, the Marine YOs had borne the brunt of a simulated armour (tank) attack – simulated in so far as the tanks hadn't actually fired live rounds. But then, they hardly needed to since the Engineers had laid explosive charges that, when detonated, mimicked perfectly the effect of tank and artillery gunfire 'walking' toward their target – that is, coming ever closer and closer. Following the artillery bombardment had come the tanks, straight through the YOs' position. Unfortunately, one of the tanks had come a shade too close to a trench – ran over part of it, in fact. The fact that trenches are designed to withstand a tank running over them, and that this trench had behaved perfectly, had been totally lost on the four YOs who'd dived into the far end, away from the tank's tracks, cursing every single tank driver who ever lived.

(A trench designed and built to withstand a tank running over it is one of the more curious concepts of the military mind. For in the battle, tanks do not quickly and politely pass over a trench. They reverse back and forth over it, swinging from one track to another, so collapsing the trench and burying its inhabitants. But a static infantry defence against an armoured attack is one of the more cherished concepts within certain defence circles.)

A hard night

The final part of the night's activities, a few hours after the live firing was over, had begun for the YOs with an eight-mile yomp, carrying all their gear, across Salisbury Plain to a rendezvous at a deserted farmhouse. Needless to say, during the last hour of their yomp the weather had turned particularly nasty. Winds gusted to forty miles an hour, bringing with them abnormally large hailstones. Hard enough at the best of times – but when you're exhausted and carrying close to a hundred pounds on your back. . . .

When they had reached the farmhouse the YOs had done what all good YOs and recruits do – found a sheltered spot and gone to sleep. Typically, one YO had been so tired that when spoken to by an instructor who wanted to know if the batch understood their instructions for the rest of the night, he had managed to answer all the questions while still asleep.

Shortly before 0300 the YOs had been woken, got their kit together and joined the army officers for a four-mile yomp to the start line for a series of troop attacks against a fortified position. That attack had been a bit of a disaster.

Enemy supposedly killed had suddenly resurrected as the YOs advanced, and attacked the Marines from behind. One YO section had disintegrated in a welter of accusation and counter-accusation, the men deciding that their commander for the night had made one mistake too many, telling him so in no uncertain terms. And all the while the instructors were following and watching, only becoming involved when things had got too much out of hand.

'Yeah, it was a bit of a shambles,' one of the instructors admitted afterwards, 'but that's what war is like. You can't figure out who's going to make a good officer until things do go badly wrong. But I was badly surprised by Mr —. He let us all down tonight.' It was said with genuine regret, almost the comment a teacher would make about a favourite pupil.

To be told that he's let everyone down is the worst rebuke a YO can receive. It implies that he's betrayed the trust placed in him, that he's unfit to be given command, and that he thinks more of himself than he does of his fellow Marines. A YO who continually lets his instructors, his batch-mates and himself down will not stay long at Lympstone.

Tricks of the trade

While YOs and recruits are naturally aware of each other's existence, they usually train together only on exercise. The YOs in particular welcome this because that's when they learn all the little tricks of keeping comfortable in the field that the instructors never seem to teach. Like, for example, taking babywipes (impregnated tissues used for cleaning babies) – so much easier to keep oneself clean.

Also, the recruits have a well-deserved reputation of knowing where and how to get the best deals on civilian manufactured equipment, bought to supplement official issue. It might be a petrol cooker, a Gortex bivvie bag (a sleeping bag cover that's waterproof yet still allows sweat vapour to escape) or even a particular brand of bergen – before the Crusader model became standard issue, recruits used to buy their own. Whatever the piece of kit, the recruit will know if it really works and how cheaply it can be bought.

By and large, however, neither YOs nor recruits are encouraged to buy their own kit until they've been at Lympstone for some time. They're not officially encouraged in the first instance, since the standard-issue equipment is, in theory, perfectly adequate for all their needs. . . .

The fact that YOs and recruits train in the same establishment begins to foster the family atmosphere that the Marines are so proud of. For Lympstone is a time of shared experiences, the time when YO and recruit alike begin to appreciate the ugly side of war . . . that it's not all *Boy's*

COMMANDO TESTS

These are the final tests that every man must successfully complete in order to win a Green Beret. They are taken in full battle-order kit weighing 30 pounds (2 stone 2 pounds), which probably weighs at least forty pounds (2 stone 12 pounds) when wet. Somehow, it always manages to get wet. Additionally, each man will also be carrying a rifle weighing just under 10 pounds.

Tarzan Course	5 minutes for recuits, 4.5 minutes for YOs
Tarzan Course and Assault Course	13 minutes for recruits, 12.5 minutes for YOs
Endurance Course, plus four-mile run back to camp	73 minutes for recruits, 70 minutes for YOs
9-mile speed march	90 minutes for all
6-mile speed march	60 minutes for all
30-mile yomp	8 hours for recruits, 7 hours for YOs
30-foot rope climb	no time limit (obviously, if it's not done in a few minutes, the man falls off)
Battle Swimming Test	no time limit – the man jumps into a pool wearing full kit, swims for 50 metres, treads water for 2 minutes, takes off kit and hands it to a man standing at the side of the pool and treads water for another 2 minutes. At no time can he touch the side of the pool

NB: After the 9-mile speed march, the men must take part in a troop attack. After the Endurance Course and run-back, they must be able to fire their rifles on the 25-metre range immediately – this is as much a test of a man's ability to keep his rifle clean as it is of his fitness and stamina.

Own fun or gung-ho heroics, but a deadly serious business. Very deadly, since soldiers are not so much taught to die for their country as to kill for it.

YO and recruit alike have it hammered home to them that, for example, the bullet from a modern rifle hits with such an impact that it will disable, even kill from shock alone. That Warsaw Pact binary chemical weapons are designed to first induce vomiting – making a soldier take off his gas mask – and then to kill him by attacking his central nervous system. That if you *have* to move through a minefield in a hurry, the best way is simply to run as fast as you can in a straight line – apparently this gives a reasonably good chance of survival, *if* the mines have been sown in a standard pattern. That if an officer is saluted on the battlefield, or his rank indicated in any way, then a sniper may well shoot him seconds later. YOs and recruits are taught that the only way to make sure that these – and all the other nasty things that can happen to a man in war – don't happen to them is by being extremely professional – and by getting their retaliation in first.

The cost of effectiveness

Long and hard as both YO and recruit training is, it's not nearly long enough. The instructors would ideally like at least two extra months tagged on to YO training and probably the same for recruit training. But the response from the powers that be appears to be to try shortening the training time even more – both courses have lost at least a month over the past five years. There are two apparent reasons for this official attitude.

First, it costs a good deal of money to keep a YO or recruit at Lympstone (a minimum of £30,000 per recruit, probably nearer £45,000 per YO). While they're at Lympstone they're not actually doing very much in terms of defending their country, so it's better to get them through training and out to their units as soon as possible.

Second, in common with all the services, the Royal Marines suffer from men deciding not to make the Corps their life career. This results, in the Corps' own case, from a lack of foreign postings; the fact that married accompanied postings are allowed only if the posting is for a year or longer – meaning many long separations; and the very efficiency and success of the Corps that results in Royal Marines spending so much time away from home with their units. It was estimated, for example, that in 1986, between a tour in Northern Ireland, winter deployment in Norway and standard training exercises, the men of 45 Commando (based in Arbroath) spent less than six weeks at home.

All of this is accompanied by the general dissatisfaction that the Corps is not given the right equipment for the job – and indeed, until George Younger, Secretary of State for Defence, went on record as saying that there *would* be replacements for HMS *Intrepid* and *Fearless* (amphibious landing command and control ships), there was some doubt as to whether the Royal Marines would survive as a separate organization.

The official answer to this manning problem appears to be to get as many men as possible through Lympstone in as short a time as possible, so making up any shortfall in unit manpower.

The instructors would probably argue with some justification that any shortening of the training syllabus will only affect the overall efficiency of the Corps. That it is unfair and impracticable to expect units to do Lympstone's job. That better man management, an attempt to make the life more attractive, would solve many of the manpower problems. As it is, the fact that the courses are not long enough means that they have to be that much more intense, both physically and mentally. Paradoxically, this results in men failing Lympstone who should have been able to pass, particularly if they suffer an injury which never has time to heal properly (an injury gained in the first instance because they're under so much pressure).

The problem appears to be that while the politicians, planners, service chiefs and civil servants in London do appreciate the Royal Marines and what they can do, they don't want to pay for them – and are too ready, on occasions, to listen to other units claiming that they are equally as effective, but at far less cost. Even though the Falklands War proved how wrong that argument is, it's still continually resurrected. And surely the point is that if the country is going to have elite troops – be they Marines, Paras, Gurkhas or whoever – it must be prepared to pay for them, and not try to do the whole thing on the cheap. Certainly elite troops have shown themselves more effective than more conventional forces – not just in the Falklands, but also in 'low-intensity' operations like Northern Ireland.

It's an argument that's slated to go on for a long time to come; and it's one that largely escapes both YO and recruit as they sweat and strain and stumble towards that magical moment when they're presented with their Green Berets as fully fledged Royal Marine Commandos.

Like all university entrants, Prince Edward had ample opportunity to discover how demanding life in the Corps could be

3/NOT SO ROYAL MARINES

Left and above: Learning to have faith in one's equipment, one's abilities and one's instructor. Below: An easy stroll for a PTI often requires others to make an all-out effort

Comes the day when all the pain and pressure seems worthwhile – the day when the successful recruit or YO is presented with his Green Beret. But many fall by the wayside. One of the most spectacular recent failures was HRH The Prince Edward

No Royal Marine ever forgets the day he passes out from Lympstone. The day he's given his Green Beret. The day – if he's a recruit – that he's referred to as *being* a Royal Marine for the first time. The day that the Adjutant's horse invariably defecates at the very moment that the King's Squad is marching past the Inspecting Officer – trying to keep a straight face at that moment is perhaps the hardest thing any man has had to do at Lympstone, never mind the Tarzan or Endurance Courses.

Pass-out day is the time when the Corps salutes the recruits – or YOs – and accepts them into its family. But of late it's also become the time when the Corps salutes the recruits' and YOs' own families because, as the Corps knows, it is very hard for a man to complete the training without the support of his family. It's usually given unstintingly, even though the family concerned may be slightly confused as to why their son – or brother or nephew or even boyfriend – wanted to be a Royal Marine in the first place.

For the families the day begins early when they arrive at the camp – for most, if not all, the first time that they've been anywhere near a military establishment. But always amongst them there's at least one father, or uncle or grandfather or simply friend of the family, bursting with pride and with the unmistakable air of the ex-Royal Marine, back amongst his companions. The families are directed to Mountbatten Hall for coffee before moving into the auditorium where they're greeted by the Officer Commanding recruit training, who introduces himself, their sons' troop officer and the instructors. The families are interested – can these be the men who've been making their sons' lives such a misery for the past six months? Why, they look so, well, normal. The OC then explains the purpose of recruit training: 'To train a man to take his place with confidence as a rifleman in a commando and as a man who understands his role as a responsible citizen.' This is followed by a brief explanation of what the training entails.

Those parents, families or friends who are total strangers to military life begin to look at each other in disbelief. Well, they'd known it was going to

The Sword of Honour – proudly received by the best Young Officer following training at Lympstone

be hard but they had no idea quite how hard, for recruits are notorious at not letting their families know the details of what they're going through – partly because they don't want to worry anyone, partly because it's difficult to discuss the course with anyone who hasn't experienced it.

So often when a recruit calls home with the news that he's thinking of leaving – which the Corps has already warned all parents to expect – the reaction is 'Stick it out, Son, for a few more days, and then decide.' If some parents had realized exactly what was involved, they might well have come down and collected the recruit themselves. For although the Corps goes to great lengths to explain to parents exactly what *is* involved, it's one thing to see the course laid out on paper, another to see a film of the Endurance Course of the thirty-miler and realize that one's own son has suffered just like the men on the screen. And those parents who were perhaps still disposed to regard the Commando Course as adventure training with discipline find real cause for pride in their sons' achievements.

A personal achievement

Finally, the curtain is raised and there are the King's Squad, dressed in combat gear and cap comforters, standing to attention and waiting to be presented with their Green Berets.

It is, perhaps, a ceremony that sounds a little bit over the top. Possibly, one would expect the recruits to be led up on to the moors and told to make their way, at night, to various isolated map references where they would find their Green Berets half way up an inaccessible crag and have to retrieve them any way they could. But this ceremony is not really for the recruits. Their ceremony comes later, on the parade ground. This is for the parents.

As each recruit's name is called he marches forward to receive his green beret. As he does so, his troop officer gives a short but fair account of how well or not so well the man did in training.

(At one recent pass-out, the ceremony was interrupted by the OC who told the audience that one particular man had managed to complete both the nine-mile speed march and the thirty-miler with a broken foot – 'One of the bravest acts I have ever seen.' Which came as a complete shock to the man's parents: 'We'd known he was injured, but he never said how badly.' In fact, he'd never told his *instructors* how badly, only his own recruit troop.)

Green Beret presentation over, there's a break while the troop rush off to change into their dress blues for the pass-out parade proper. Meanwhile the parents begin to chat amiably with the instructors – even those parents who, perhaps, only a few months ago had threatened to call upon their MPs, Amnesty International or even the European Court of Human Rights if their son was not allowed to leave as he wished. For the sheer look of pride on the young man's face as he received his Green Beret had been enough to prove that a case can be made for making a recruit stay and tough it out. For some recruits it is the first difficult achievement of their lives. As one mother said: 'I don't totally agree with what he's doing – but it has made him a more responsible boy and made him much more self-confident. So I'm thankful for that much, at least.'

The moment of truth
The King's Squad on parade is a very emotive sight. With the Royal Marines Band playing to one side, the men march and countermarch. They may not have had very long to practise – drill does not feature much during the last five weeks of the course – but, as the programme says, they are to give a demonstration of discipline, pride and unity as a troop. The parade always attracts the attention of passers-by, of Royal Marines who stand there for a few minutes reliving memories of their own passing-out parade . . . or perhaps of men they've served with or commanded.

'I never ever grow tired of watching this,' said one Royal Marine officer quietly, his voice full of pride in the Corps and most of all, pride in the young Marines who've elected to join his family.

'Royal Marines, to your duties quick march' orders the Inspecting Officer and to the tune of 'Auld Lang Syne' and 'Sarie Marias' the troop marches off. Shortly to join the families and instructors for a celebratory drink.

It is then that the downside of parental pride shows itself. When, faced with a son still resplendent in Dress Blues – a son grown more confident, more mature (and even more caring, as a sister rather wonderingly said) – a parent also has to face the prospect of their son being killed or injured in battle. Or killing or injuring someone else in battle.

One can explain to parents that war only happens as a last resort, that the better trained and equipped the country's forces are, the less likely that war will occur. The Falklands War put the lie to that argument for war knows no logic, and Marines more than most soldiers are trained to handle the sudden and the unexpected.

'It's what he wants to do,' a mother says, 'and I'll support him – but I'll always worry about him. What mother wouldn't?' And not for the first time it occurs that it takes as much courage for some to stay behind as it does for others to go and fight.

It's at this time, too, that it's possible to gain some inkling of how much Lympstone changes a man. Parents remark on how much much more mature a son has become, how more helpful about the house, how much more positive. But many also remark on how their son has lost contact with his old friends, that he appears to have less in common with them – which is something that the young Marines themselves have noticed.

'I just find all my old mates really trivial,' said one, 'not interested in doing much with their lives.'

But the truth is a little more complicated than that. Lympstone does not exist to change a man from street-corner yobbo to respectful, committed member of society. It might try to teach him a little natural respect; it will use any commitment he has to get him through training; it does teach him responsibility and self-confidence – but only because those values are consistent with his job as a Royal Marine. And since recruits are young, and by definition slightly extremist, they embrace the ethos of the Corps wholeheartedly. For some it's almost like a religious conversion – and as has often been remarked, a religious convert is usually keener than someone brought up in the same faith. So perhaps this isolation from childhood friends is a little contrived, or as much the result of the intensity of feeling that exists within a recruit troop, as it is of any miraculous personality change. For the paradox is, as the Marine himself will find, that the longer he stays in the Corps, the more he will want to develop a 'civilian' life divorced from his job as a Royal Marine. But that is all in the future. For now, as yesterday's recruit basks in the congratulations of family and instructors, he can be forgiven for his somewhat blinkered approach to life, for his belief that only Royal Marines matter. After all, it is that belief born of commitment that got him through training.

Not like the rest of us
For every man, YO or recruit, who completes Lympstone, there are at least five who failed – and at least thirty who were denied the very opportunity. One of the more spectacular failures in recent years was HRH The Prince Edward . . . a failure in the Corps' eyes at least, since it wanted him to pass so very, very much. Perhaps a little too much, in so far as the question remains whether he should have been considered as a Royal Marine in the first place. But over and above the embarrassment his going caused, the Corps felt the same loss as it would of any YO or recruit, and immediately asked the question: 'What went wrong – and could we have prevented it, and can we prevent a similar situation in the future?'

When Prince Edward first announced his intention of joining the Royal Marines, the Corps had been delighted. For the presence of a Royal within its ranks would undoubtedly help with the political infighting within Whitehall. The Corps was also somewhat flattered that a young man with such an assured future should choose to become a Marine – and sentimentally pleased that the son of the Corps Captain General (Prince Philip) and the great nephew of the Corps' most stalwart defender (Lord Louis Mountbatten) should want to win a Green Beret. However, it was made plain at the very outset that no exceptions could be made, that Prince Edward would have to pass out from Lympstone having done everything, and to the same standard, that is required of any YO.

It can't be argued that Prince Edward didn't know what he was letting himself in for. Like every other university entrant, he spent time with the Corps during the vacations. He drove rigid raiders (small fast boats) on the rivers in Belize, camped out in the wet and cold on Exmoor. His commitment apparently undiminished, he joined Lympstone in September, 1986. Which is when the problems really began.

At the Palace's insistence, there was to be no publicity whatsoever surrounding the prince's time in training – save for one brief photo call on the day he joined. Thereafter, the camp was to be closed to nearly all comers. No visiting press whatsoever was allowed in, other than those previously sanctioned, or those in pursuit of a story that palpably had nothing to do with Prince Edward. Journalists allowed inside were by and large 'minded off', i.e. kept as far away from the prince as possible. Security on the camp was tightened to an unpleasant degree, and not only to guard against possible terrorist attack. For it sometimes appears that the authorities regard the press with far more distrust, and dislike, than they do the IRA. All this was, naturally, a red rag to the press bull.

Photographers lurked in every bush, perched in every tree surrounding the camp (two being discovered, and removed at the point of a shotgun, by a local farmer). Attempts were made to bribe civilian and military staff working in the camp for any story whatsoever about Prince Edward. The quoted rate for an 'embarrassing' shot of him – say falling flat on his face in the mud – was anything up to £50,000, depending on syndication rights. For a really embarrassing shot – say Prince Edward naked and full frontal in the shower – the figure of £100,000 was bandied about. And the tighter the security, the greater the press's determination to get the story or photo.

It would have been easier and better simply to flood the press with as many Prince Edward stories as humanly possible until the entire thing became boring and a total non-event. Press releases saying the 'Prince Edward Blows Own Nose'; 'Prince Edward Falls Over'; 'Prince Edward Has Hair Cut' would eventually have driven the story out of the papers. As it was, the increased media coverage could only serve to underline the fact that royalty, like the rich, are not like the rest of us.

The fact that Prince Edward was permanently accompanied by his own police bodyguard could only serve to isolate him further. Frankly, many Marines saw the presence of a police bodyguard as being both stupid and insulting, since no British police bodyguard could protect the prince as well as a Marine, say, who belonged to that branch of the Royal Marines Police who provide bodyguards for ambassadors in political hot spots like Beirut – and for many British VIPs visiting those same hot spots.

The official reason given for the prince having a police bodyguard is that only police are allowed to carry guns as a matter of course in Britain.

However, dispensations are and have been given by the Home Office whenever the armed forces are involved in an anti-terrorist operation in Britain, which probably happens rather more than the general public realizes.

None the less, Prince Edward appeared to be doing quite well in training. Perhaps not quite up to Sword of Honour (presented to the best YO) standard that an optimistic – or mischievous – Corps spokesman once claimed. But good enough that few, if any, foresaw any problems.

True, when he hurt his knee in the second month of training his enthusiasm diminished slightly, but that was only to be expected. And while he was no longer known as 'smartass' by the instructors (due to his habit of wanting to answer every question and usually being able to do so), Prince Edward was making steady progress – his new nickname, Steady Eddie, summed it all up. However, there was one warning sign that perhaps, with hindsight, should have been spotted earlier. Prince Edward appeared to be a somewhat solitary young man – even slightly lonely. He appeared to find it a little difficult to mix in with the rest of his batch.

This is not to suggest that a Royal Marine Officer must be a total extrovert. That he has to like all his fellow YOs. That he should want to spend all his time in their company. Anyone like that would probably – and rightly – be regarded with a certain degree of suspicion, since most YOs – as do recruits – feel the need to get away on their own from time to time. But unless a YO, as has already been said, does become an integral part of his batch, he will not pass the course. More to the point, he won't want to pass the course: again, there are times when the only thing that gets a man through is loyalty to, a sense of belonging to, the group. Whether or not you like half the people in that group is beside the point. You pass as a group or not at all.

But one of the problems that sometimes face graduate entrants to Lympstone is that they find it a little more difficult to make contact with their fellow YOs than do non-graduates. Possibly because they're already in the wrong frame of mind since, having completed three years of study, they're faced with yet another year. Possibly because those three years count for very little at Lympstone, have very little relevance to passing a commando course. Possibly because they can't bridge the intellect gap between graduate and non-graduate. Possibly because graduates tend to be a little older than the rest. Whatever the reason, graduates do sometimes stand out from their batch, remaining somewhat aloof. But that wasn't what appeared to have happened in Prince Edward's case.

Prince Edward also appeared to have a problem in that he apparently wanted to be far better at training than he actually was. Perhaps he felt that his position made it incumbent on him to be one of the best, if not *the* best. Not only does an attitude like this add to the pressure a man's already experiencing, it can also be slightly annoying for the rest of the YOs. The situation then worsens when the man feels hurt and confused by the refusal of his fellow YOs to take him at his own evaluation. And so he becomes even more isolated and begins to resent the very men who represent his only hope of becoming an officer in the Royal Marines: yet again, he can't do it without them.

This suggests that Prince Edward's motivation for joining the Corps was less than he simply wanted to be a Marine, more that he possibly had some

Happier times – Prince Edward in Royal Marines blues rides with the Duke of York to Westminster Abbey for his brother's wedding

sort of Young Lochinvar complex. If so, he wasn't the first and won't be the last. It is very easy for any young man to become infatuated with the image of himself as a Commando if he's thinking of joining the services. If he has a strong theatrical streak running through him (as Prince Edward appears to have) it's easy, gratifying and fun to see himself winning a Green Beret (something that Edward's two elder brothers never did) and then becoming involved in deeds of derring-do.

There can be few worse reasons for wanting to join the Royal Marines. No way will this type of motivation hold up on Dartmoor in the wintertime. For while a sense of the dramatic or a streak of romanticism can't do any harm, the reality of becoming a Marine demands a greater commitment than play-acting or wishful thinking provide.

(And if that is the case, perhaps Prince Edward should be congratulated for staying as long as he did.)

Reconsidering his future

YOs have two weeks' leave at Christmas. Very few of them want to come back to Lympstone. They'd be less than human if they did want to swap the warmth and comfort of home for a leaky brushwood bivvy, or their own bed for a damp sleeping bag that's invariably lying on the sharpest stones in the country.

(One YO did tell of a batch-mate who actually appeared to enjoy all the phases of training, who even went on a mud run – a punishment run through estuary mud – just to see what it was like, and altogether 'had the sort of attitude that gives YOs a bad name'.)

Every time there is a long leave, at least one YO will call up and say he's thinking of not coming back. At this point his OC – who's heard it all before – will say fine, we do understand, but come back anyway and let's talk about it. And the YO does, and usually ends up rejoining his batch. Every – but every – YO wants to leave Lympstone at some time or another. One man spent a month writing out his resignation several times a day.

'If that's what it takes to keep him in,' said his instructor, 'we don't care – he can write his resignation every hour if he likes. It's just his way of coping with the pressure.'

YOs have other ways of letting off steam – ways that are built into the course itself. The sergeant major of the officer training wing often finds himself dispensing as much fatherly as military advice, since YOs may find it easier to talk to him than to their instructors, if they find it hard to cope with the demands made upon them.

Then, each YO at Lympstone is 'adopted' by a married officer and his family, an officer who works at the camp but is totally unconnected with officer training. This provides the YO with a domestic environment in which he can admit to his worries and insecurities – and find that they're probably identical to those his 'godfather' felt when he was going through officer training. But no one can force a YO to avail himself of this built-in counselling service, any more than they can force a YO to talk about his problems with the rest of his batch.

Certainly, the news that Prince Edward was 'reconsidering his future in the Corps', as the Palace statement rather coyly had it, came as a complete shock to all at Lympstone – although there were one or two officers who said that they'd never really seen him as a troop member. But this was probably being wise after the event.

Again, there was nothing particularly strange in Prince Edward wanting to stay home. Where the episode did begin to lurch into the tragi-comedy that it ultimately became was when the Commandant General (the senior Royal Marine) was summoned to the Palace in an attempt to talk Prince Edward out of his decision. Not many recalcitrant YOs are interviewed by the Commandant General and once again – as with the media interest, the bodyguards – it became apparent that the prince was a special case and had been accorded special treatment, however much he wanted to be treated like any other YO. Who just happened to be fifth in line to the throne.

There was nothing strange about the 'counselling' process that the prince then underwent. The Corps had spent a good deal of money on him already and dislikes losing potential officers. The Corps also wanted to know what had gone wrong, if only to learn lessons for the future. So this 'counselling' process is applied when any promising YO wants to quit. For the Corps also knows that many YOs have quit only to regret it later, have written saying that if only someone had managed to talk them out of their decision, how much happier they would now be. Unfortunately the impression the press gave was that the prince was being subjected to special 'counselling', that the Corps was doing everything in its power, short of kidnap, to keep him within its ranks. Whereas the attitude of the vast number of Marines was, that if he didn't want to stay, then let him leave. And the sooner the better.

It was a time of leak and counter leak to the press. Most of the leaking was done by the Palace, who saw as their first duty the protection of Prince Edward's name and reputation, even at the expense of the Royal Marines, who by and large maintained a dignified and frustrated silence despite being stabbed in the back by journalists and other service units who should have known better.

The accepted explanation became that Prince Edward – a sensitive, intelligent, cultivated and oh! so very non-macho (feminist writers loved that one) young man – had not so very surprisingly fallen out with a brutal regime, notable for its unintelligent approach to life in general (and according to an unnamed SAS officer, war in particular), its regimentation, its domination by sergeants and dislike for the academic (that from a one-time lecturer at Sandhurst who had his own axe to grind). Small wonder that such a paragon of modern princely virtues had come to his senses, and what took him so long?

Aside from the fact that two A levels and a second-class history degree, even from Cambridge, are hardly an indication of superior intelligence, the regime is not brutal. Marines are not noted for their lack of intelligence nor are they particularly macho (ask their wives).

Sergeants do have a good deal of responsibility, more so than say in the Brigade of Guards, and can present a formidable challenge to a weak or unprofessional officer merely by being so good at their jobs. The Corps does not dislike the academic by any means, as we have seen. And the authorized version of Prince Edward's decision to reconsider his future totally ignored his earlier commitment to finish his training at Lympstone if he were physically capable of doing so – as he was.

It had been made plain to the prince that whatever happened, he was expected to do his damnedest to win a Green Beret. Little else other than a supreme effort on his part could justify the trouble already taken to accommodate him both as a prince and as a university graduate (graduate entrants are paid during their time at university; although they must pay this money back if they resign before completing a minimum of five years). The time to reconsider one's future in the Corps is after training, not before it – unless a man is so obviously incompetent that his resignation comes as a sweet relief to all concerned.

However, given the media pressure on the prince it was hardly surprising that he decided to resign, although up until the very last moment his instructors thought that he'd reconsider and finish the year.

'It won't affect him now,' said a journalist who knows the Corps well, 'but it may well do so in a few years' time. It's very easy for anyone going through that training to find all sorts of reasons why they should quit. Maybe some of those reasons are right, who knows? But some time he's going to ask himself if he could have done it. It's not what other people think of him, it's what he thinks of himself that'll matter. I think he should have finished the course. As it was, he left an awful lot of people feeling badly let down.'

Meanwhile, the Corps had been bracing itself for the first T-shirts made up by the less reverential marines to appear:

'NOT by Royal Appointment'

'NOT SO ROYAL MARINES'

'Royal Marines Go Where Princes Fear to Tread'

'I couldn't make it as a Prince . . . so I became a Royal Marine'

And within days, special leave applications were flooding in to company officers, asking for 'time to reconsider my future in the Corps'. It's as well that Marines know how to laugh at themselves.

In retrospect

If there are any lessons to be learnt, they're fairly obvious ones:

— That YOs should not be allowed to resign during training – although this would probably affect the entire rank structure in the armed forces, since officers may resign (within reason) whenever they like.

— That if a prince of the Royal Household ever again joins the Corps, it's on the understanding that the Corps is responsible for everything – publicity, bodyguards etc. – and that the prince acts exactly like any other YO, i.e. withdraws completely from royal duties while he's at Lympstone.

— That the Royal Marines should reconsider the whole position of university entrants – and possibly train them *before* they go to university.

— That the Corps does try to screen its potential officers in such a way that any personality problems will come to the fore that much sooner – a little less emphasis on being an officer pure and simple and a little more on being an officer in the Royal Marines might help.

— That the training is extended to alleviate unnecessary pressure.

And finally, that the Corps as a whole stops its 'close-ranks' attitude when faced with media pressure or the hint of a scandal. For no matter how well meant, the silence from the Corps while Prince Edward was agonizing over his future did little to help.

4/THE SPECIALISTS

An Assault Engineer (Specialist) and a Sniper (Adqual) demonstrate a small part of their skill – details overleaf

Part of the uniqueness of the Royal Marines lies in the Corps' ability to handle a wide variety of military jobs – an ability born of its determination to be as self-contained as possible. To illustrate that facet of the Corps, here is a brief look at a few of its specializations

Royal Marines are encouraged to gain either a Specialist Qualification (SQ) or Technical Qualification (TQ). There are twenty-eight SQs and TQs altogether, and promotion beyond the rank of sergeant is blocked unless one or the other has been obtained. Officers may also gain certain SQs or TQs, such as an ML (Mountain Leader) or an SC (Swimmer Canoeist – Special Boat Service) or a Helicopter Pilot (predominantly an Officer's SQ); but many of the branches are closed to officers simply because they do not have the time to learn that particular trade. They are, after all, theoretically being trained for senior command positions.

A few SQs and TQs are unique to the Corps; all are unique in the way the Corps both emphasizes them and makes them self-regulating, responsible for maintaining the professional standards within the branch with the minimum of outside supervision.

It's not possible to cover all the branches in detail, for each SQ and TQ probably deserves a book to itself. And before talking about the few that have been chosen, it should be explained that no matter what his SQ or TQ, the man is first and foremost expected to be a combat-ready Marine; that a sergeant Armourer, say, is still expected to be able to take on the job of troop sergeant should it ever be necessary – as is a sergeant Clerk or a sergeant Cook. Admittedly the chances are remote, but the principle remains – even if it's not always personally adhered to in terms of, say, physical fitness.

There are so many SQs and TQs because the Royal Marines insist on being as self-sufficient as possible. Marines themselves fulfil many of the functions that in the army are undertaken by specialist corps. Two that they can't do account for the presence within 3 Commando Brigade of 29 Commando Regiment Royal Artillery and 59 Commando Regiment Royal Engineers. But everything else must be done by the Royal Marines.

Drill Leaders (DLs – NCOs only)
The Royal Marines would probably be the first to agree that drill for drill's sake has little or no relevance to modern warfare. Ceremonial parades may

look grand, but unless they have some relevance to the job in hand, they're largely a waste of time and money. Worse, they may even detract from a soldier's ability to fight and survive on the battlefield, since a man trained only to respond to and operate within a rigid chain of command will suffer if a link in that chain is killed.

So for the Royal Marines, drill and ceremonial are merely the outward signs of self-discipline and high personal standards. To be more specific, to the Corps drill is the 'cold face of discipline' – initially, the discipline instilled in a man before he can begin to learn the self-discipline that the Corps values so highly. Responsible for instilling that initial discipline are the Drill Leaders – the men who 'mother' recruit and YO alike through the first difficult weeks of training.

As well as teaching their charges how to march and salute, the Corps traditions and history, the DLs also teach recruit and YO how to look after themselves. How to wash and iron their clothes. How to keep themselves clean in the worst conditions; to take pride in their personal appearance not only because it looks good on parade, but because it's a boost to morale, particularly in the field.

DLs are born, not made. It takes a special kind of person, one who wants to communicate his own enthusiasm for the Corps in such a way that he can fire the imaginations of the men he's responsible for. Most if not all DLs are 'Corps pissed', as the Marines say, meaning a man who is totally in love with the Corps and his job within it. As witness the fact that progress through his branch is left very much up to the man himself. While there are courses he takes before promotion to corporal or sergeant, he is expected to do much of the work beforehand, in his own time.

For most men who've been in the army, their memories of drill instructors distil down to a loud, well-creased voice that squawked, screamed and squeaked its way into their dreams. Royal Marine DLs, however, do not believe in shouting on parade. They'll spend many hours practising voice projection so that they can make themselves heard without frightening everyone within earshot.

And as to whether it's all worth it? During the Korean War, elements of a USMC division were in retreat from Choisin Reservoir, and 41 (Independent) Commando was sent to help them get back to the safety of the UN lines. The US Marines were openly impressed at the way the men of 41 Commando marched and generally deported themselves; with how they managed to remain neat and clean in the worst conditions; and how their self-discipline helped to turn what could have been a rout into a successful retreat – or tactical withdrawal, in correct military parlance. Those attributes of self-discipline and pride in oneself and one's corps are initially taught to Marines by the DL Branch – who also see themselves as continually responsible for overall standards within the Corps.

Platoon Weapons (PWs – NCOs only)
Corps folklore has it that most PWs took so long to decide on an SQ or TQ that their minds were made up for them by higher authority and they ended up in the PW Branch. This slightly unkind attitude is probably due to the fact that PWs are responsible for most of the YO and recruit training at Lympstone – and few Royal Marines enjoy their time at

Lympstone. PWs also supervise the Junior and Senior Command Courses that have to be passed before promotion to corporal or sergeant. Overall they are responsible for the standard of infantry skills within the Corps. As such, they spend a good deal of their time telling others what they've done wrong. But the PW Branch also organizes sniper training (of which more later) and is the authority on all individual weapons within the Corps. PWs teach men how to shoot and how to read a map. They are, as one said, one of the few branches that actually sees an end product from their work (at Lympstone) – the recruit or YO who's successfully completed his training – a claim that can also be made by both the DLs and the PTI Branch.

PWs are also responsible for organizing live firing, on a closed or open range. Although in theory officers are also taught range work, in practice the job is invariably given to the nearest PW. In an age of more and more esoteric specialization (clerks are now expected to master computer programming, for example) some PWs feel that they're not quite so appreciated as they would like. The problem is that the total professionalism of the branch has come to be expected to such a degree that PWs are taken for granted. Also, because PWs are responsible for so much that is basic to the making of a Royal Marine, the smallest mistake that a PW makes (even, for example, confusing northings and eastings on a map reference) is gleefully seized upon by other Marines with less than happy memories of life as a recruit.

Good Drill Leaders need to be extroverts, to dominate by force of personality

Without taking anything away from senior NCOs, PW corporals are probably the most important members of the branch. Corporals in the Corps as a whole have tremendous responsibility and the PW corporals at Lympstone are responsible for most of the day-to-day training of the recruits, working closely with them under the direction of the team leader (a PW sergeant) and troop officer.

Snipers (Additional Qualification, or Adqual – officers and other ranks)
In theory, the sniper's course is the basic PW course – the one a man must first pass in order to gain further promotion within the PW Branch. In practice, because the sniper's course is to such a high standard (Royal Marine snipers are the best in the Atlantic Alliance, among the best in the world) it has the highest failure rate of any course in the Corps. For that reason, sniping is not regarded as being an SQ or TQ, but as an Adqual (additional qualification) in the same way as is completing a parachute course.

How and why the Royal Marines developed sniping as a tour-de-force explains a good deal about how the Corps thinks and operates. Although sniping had proved its value down through the centuries – in the Civil War many officers brought their gamekeepers from their own estates into battle to fulfil the sniper's role – at the end of the Second World War sniping fell into disrepute. The new scenario called for a massive Warsaw Pact armoured advance to be met by a massive NATO armoured counter-attack. Plainly there was no room for a sniper on that juggernaut-dominated battleground, and the British Army more or less forgot about them. At that point Britain became involved in a series of 'low-intensity operations', as Sir Frank Kitson dubbed them, in places like Kenya, Aden, Korea (more of a full-scale war, that one), Malaysia, Borneo and, latterly, Northern Ireland. These were basically infantry wars – as was the Falklands – demanding exceptional infantry skills. Amongst those skills is sniping. In a conventional war a sniper is trained to dominate the ground between opposing troops. His targets are any men engaged on a specialist task (an officer, signaller, heavy-weapons crew etc.) whose loss will cause even more disruption and dismay than is normal on a battlefield. A sniper is also trained to lay down harassing fire at distances of up to 1000 metres. This means that all the opposition keep their heads down, greatly adding to the confusion. Snipers are also trained to infiltrate behind enemy lines, or 'stay-behind' if the enemy advances, to try to shoot senior enemy commanders.

In unconventional war, say in Northern Ireland, snipers are extremely effective at hiding up, sometimes for days on end, and killing known terrorists; or in covering demonstrations or riots when it can be reasonably expected that a terrorist sniper will also be present.

So snipers do have an extremely important part to play, notwithstanding the dreams of the technocrats, planners and cavalry. As luck – and good foresight – had it, the Royal Marines had insisted on keeping their own sniping skills alive and well after the Second World War, since they saw them as integral to commando-style operations – yet another example of the Corps going its own way and ultimately being proved right. (A similar situation arose with the creation of the Mountain Leaders Branch.)

As it was, the Royal Marines were in a position to pass on their skills, not only to the British Army but also to the USMC who modelled their sniper's course on Lympstone's. The irony of it all is that the Argentinian snipers who posed some problems during the Falklands War may well have been trained by the USMC. Certainly they were probably the recipients of training methods that originated with the Royal Marines.

Where the sniper's course at Lympstone (lasting some six weeks) differs from the British Army's sniper training is that the Royal Marines centralize all training at Lympstone, whereas the Army trains sniper instructors, who then go back to their own units and train their own regimental snipers. Obviously this type of approach can only result, over a period, in a dilution of standards. But with centralized control the Corps can ensure that standards remain as high as ever. So all Royal Marine snipers are trained at Lympstone, together with a few selected police officers and some army personnel. Less than forty-five per cent of all men taking the course pass completely – a figure that does not include police attendances, since policemen are less concerned with the military aspects of sniping. None the less, the sniper's course is one of the very few that will make a man a better soldier even if he fails. Often, a man who does fail the course will become a sniper's number two – the man often responsible for providing protection for the sniper himself.

The Corps claims that there is no reason why any trained Marine should not be able to pass the sniper's course. But then, it claims exactly the same for the SC3 course (SBS) and the ML2 course (Mountain Leaders). What they really mean is that the course starts at the standard of the trained Marine and goes on from there – no special preparation is needed in the first instance. A sniper does not even have to be a natural shot – shooting can be learnt. But he does have to be a natural soldier to whom fieldcraft

Royal Marine Assault Engineers teaching mine clearance techniques on *Canberra*

Overleaf: River crossings are also the responsibility of the Assault Engineers Branch. All the Marines are wearing gas-inflatable life jackets

comes easily. He must have a natural awareness of his surroundings and the ability to merge into the background, which probably explains why most snipers, even those who operate well in an urban environment, were born and raised in the country. Finally, contrary to popular opinion, snipers do not have a favourite rifle. That is to say, they are not encouraged to have their own personal weapons, for the very good reason that a man who places too much faith in a particular weapon will not be effective if anything happens to it. He will have forgotten that a rifle by itself possesses no special skills – those belong to the man who uses it. Similarly, when Marines first go on the course and are issued with their gilly suits – combat gear covered with strips of cloth – they tend to add all manner of leaves and grass in the field. Later, as their confidence in their own ability increases, they tend to discard most of the foliage since a gilly suit by itself will hide a man who knows how to take full advantage of any cover that's available.

Assault Engineers (AEs – NCOs only)

The Assault Engineers are unique to the Royal Marines. While there is a permanent unit of commando-trained Royal Engineers (men who've completed a five-week All Arms Commando Course, run independently of recruit training), and while the Marines are positive that the men of 59 Squadron RE are the best in the business (Marines are inordinately proud of both the Royal Engineers and the Royal Artillery units who choose to serve with them), the Corps has found it necessary to maintain its own military engineering capability, operating at troop or company level. Whereas 59 Squadron deal mainly with heavy plant equipment, most of the Assault Engineer's kit is either man-portable or can be carried on a Land-Rover or three-tonner – or, occasionally, lifted into place by a Sea King helicopter.

Assault Engineers are expected to undertake a variety of tasks, ranging from establishing fresh-water supplies to sowing a minefield, or clearing one; from building or blowing up a bridge, to overseeing the building of trenches strong enough to withstand an artillery bombardment, with one shell landing every five square metres (one shell in every area measuring seven and a half by six feet); to setting up booby traps, to training others how to disarm them. Assault Engineers are also trained coxswains, since theirs is the branch responsible for river crossings. There are never any more than fifty or sixty Assault Engineers scattered throughout the Corps, possibly because promotion within the branch tends to be slow. Some AEs have had to wait for up to six years for the course they must take in order to be promoted to sergeant.

Possibly their versatility is best illustrated by the AE colour sergeant who was pressed into service by the Royal Engineers in the Falklands to help defuse a mass of unexploded Argentinian shells. He'd never done the job before, but after a quick on-the-spot training programme (and how many men get to train on live shells?) he started work, winning the British Empire Medal in the process.

Illustrators (NCOs and Non-ranking Marines only)

Unlike DLs, PWs and AEs, the Illustrators Branch trains at Royal Marines Poole, the Corps' other major training establishment.

Illustrators, a comparatively recent innovation within the Corps, are one of the smallest branches. Formed in 1968, the branch numbers only twenty-one (only the Grooms Branch, numbering twelve and the now-defunct Air (helicopter) Gunners Branch, which numbered four at the most, could claim to be smaller). The Illustrators provide many skills that used to be supplied by attached Royal Engineers and Intelligence Corps NCOs from the Army, since one of their functions is producing detailed maps and plans using air photographs – Illustrators are very heavily involved with Operational, or Combat, Intelligence. They also work very closely with the SBS and with Comacchio Group; should an oil rig or a ship be hijacked, it would be the responsibility of an Illustrator to produce an extremely accurate scale model so that the Marines could plan their rescue operation in detail and with greater confidence. Similarly, in conventional warfare, the Illustrators are responsible for producing a three-dimensional model of the terrain over which the commander is planning to attack. For however accurate, maps can never tell the complete story – a model helps to put the sitation into perspective in a very positive sense. Illustrators are also responsible for designing most of the printed material that the Corps produces internally – working closely with the Printers Branch – and while this material includes the inevitable invitations and mess menus, they do have to show a reasonably artistic flair. Illustrators are trained to first-year art college standard in graphic design, illustration and drawing – it's slightly surprising when talking to them to hear a man discuss the relative values and beauty of typefaces in the same breath as he'll discuss the merits of the new SA80 rifle versus the old SLR.

Carpenters (NCOs and Non-ranking Marines only)

Time was, a Royal Marines officer sadly reminisced, that you could get a house built and a car completely refurbished by using all the existing trades within the Corps. But the Upholsterers Branch, for example, is long gone – and possibly the Carpenters and Metalsmiths (see below) are the only reminders of those days when the Corps was truly self-contained.

The Carpenters Branch is one of those that many Royal Marines join when they're a little tired of all that yomping they have to do in a commando unit; and when they're beginning to think of learning some sort of trade that will be of value when they leave the Corps. It's hard to figure out who they equate to in the army. The Royal Engineers do also have a Carpenters Branch, but men from this branch are never as closely integrated within a unit as the Marine chippies obviously are within their own Corps.

Carpenters, who also train at RM Poole, teach not only their own branch but also the Assault Engineers. It may sound trite to say that the Carpenters Branch knows all there is to know about wood, but it comes pretty close to the mark. For before a man begins to learn about different carpentry techniques and how they relate to warfare, he learns about the different timbers he may have to use one day. In war, a chippy may find himself in tasks ranging from fixing semi-permanent housing, to hastily constructing duckboards. Aside from war, the Carpenters Branch is responsible for much of the upkeep of the Marines' permanent bases.

RNLMC in action
Far left: Advancing through a smoke screen, a Dutch Marine with the issue Uzzi machine gun. Left: Two 'Cloggies' take a break in Scotland – note the Dragon anti-tank rocket. Below left: Firing live mortar rounds in the Dutch Antilles. Right: Formal parade in Rotterdam. Below right: Dutch Marines move forward to secure the perimeter while the troop stores are being unloaded

Metalsmiths (NCOs and Non-ranking Marines only)

Also trained at RM Poole, the Metalsmiths Branch turns its hand to a variety of tasks ranging from repairing the side of a landing craft to mending the front mudguard of a motorbike. The branch also shows a surprising skill at decorative wrought-iron work – surprisingly because this is not necessarily the type of skill that one associates with the Royal Marines. Nevertheless, the pleasure is very real when you can walk into a workshop at Poole and discover a row of ornate metal lamps that will surround the Commando Memorial at Lympstone. It's not just that this represents a saving, but it's also fitting that the Corps should do as much work on that project as it can itself.

The standard that these last two trades (more easily recognized in the civilian sector) attain is very high. Carpenters have to master not only the more rough and ready side of their trade, but also the full range of intricate joins that any civilian carpenter needs to know. Similarly, any Marine metalsmith could take his place with confidence in most civilian factories and workshops – the old cliché about joining the services to gain a trade holds good for these two branches.

But perhaps a little sadly, both are under attack. There is an ever-increasing pressure on the Corps to allow that kind of job to be done by army personnel – or indeed, to civilianize them altogether. Already the Printers Branch has been told to cut its numbers by half; it can only be a matter of time before the beady eye of an accountant or planner in Whitehall observes those lesser-known branches within the Corps and decides that they are an expensive anachronism. Whether they are or not is largely a matter of personal judgement, based on practical experience. And while it can be argued that many of the Corps' branches belonged to more leisurely and far-flung times (and that, since the Corps is now permanently based in the UK, there is not quite the same need to carry so many different skills with it) it is a fact that you never find out how much you need a particular skill until you lose it. The lesson of the snipers should be uppermost in everyone's mind.

It has not been possible to mention all the SQs, TQs and even Adquals in any detail. Those that have been mentioned were chosen on a personal judgement that they sum up much of what is unique about the corps. Undoubtedly there will be many people who'll disagree with the choice, and to those who do, apologies.

The Royal Netherlands Marine Corps – RNLMC

It's not possible to write about the Royal Marines without mentioning the Royal Netherlands Marine Corps, for the following reasons.

The RNLMC was founded the year after the Royal Marines (1664 and 1665). They share the same battle honour – that of the capture and defence of Gibraltar in 1704. The Dutch Marines were also the last enemy troops to land on British soil (an action that took place in 1666 during the British/Dutch Wars, commemorated by their battle honour 'Chatham').

Though the relationship between the two units over the centuries has ranged from best of enemies to best of friends, they work together today in an unparalleled manner. It is the joint United Kingdom/Netherlands

RNLMC helicopters landing in Norway during a white-out (visibility twenty yards maximum)

Amphibious Force that is charged with the first reinforcement of NATO's northern flank. An RNLMC unit – Whisky Company – is permanently attached to 45 Commando at Arbroath. And much as the average Royal Marine complains about the Cloggies' appetites (and sometimes the length of their hair) the relationship between the two corps is extremely close. One of the major differences between the two forces is that the RNLMC has a high percentage of conscripts in its ranks. But the majority of Dutch Marines who serve with 3 Commando Brigade are none the less career soldiers.

One other point: in talking to the Royal Marines about this book, I was continuously asked: 'You are going to mention the Cloggies, aren't you? You can't not talk about them, they're part of us, really.' Doubtless the RNLMC will have their own views on whether they are actually part of the Royal Marines – doubtless, too, they'll appreciate the compliment.

5/
RM POOLE

Fulfilling the role of a university to Lympstone's sixth-form college, Royal Marines Poole is of equal importance as a training establishment to the efficiency of the Corps, and helps to keep alive its maritime traditions, experience and capabilities

The truth is, not many Royal Marines like Lympstone. With its major responsibilities for YO and recruit training; for Senior and Junior NCO Command Courses and for the All Arms Commando Course, it is possibly a little too regimental – it has to be. It also carries certain memories for all Marines – ones that they're proud to hold, but don't like to be reminded of to any great extent: to the Marine, Lympstone is indelibly associated with being either a yo-yo or a nod.

But Royal Marines Poole – now that is a little different. For although it's the Corps' other major training establishment, it's altogether far more relaxed. Since it's responsible for specialist training, it receives only fully trained Marines – other than YOs or recruits on short landing-craft or SBS briefings. The atmosphere is totally different. As a Royal Australian Navy officer said, one of the more noticeable facts about Poole is that when you're saluted by someone junior to yourself, it's always with a cheerful 'good morning' or 'afternoon'. Plenty of eye contact, as often as not a smile and as much a way of saying hello as anything else. Whereas saluting at Lympstone tends to be far more strictly regimental.

Royal Marines Poole trains landing-craft personnel, swimmer canoeists (SBS), ships' detachments, Royal Marine divers and various technical trades like Carpenters, Illustrators and Metalsmiths. It also trains Royal Marine Drivers – their branch, with over seven hundred men, is the biggest in the Corps. And for Trivial Pursuit freaks, Poole is the second largest natural harbour in the world, the largest being Sydney, Australia. Though advanced training courses are run at Lympstone – like the Assault Engineers and Signallers – it can't ever achieve the same atmosphere as Poole – for Poole isn't only more relaxed, it's also more quietly purposeful.

Royal Marine landing craft

For most people the Royal Marines are synonymous with landing craft – with men leaping into the sea and battling their way through waves and bullets to the beach. The official term for that type of operation is an opposed landing – and while the Corps does train for opposed landings, it doesn't like them one little bit. For whereas the amphibious armoured personnel carriers used by the USMC can – in theory – provide a high degree of protection, at least against small-arms fire, only the very largest of the landing craft used by the Royal Marines can do the same – and even then, a .50-calibre machine-gun bullet has the unhappy ability to go through quite thick armour plate. It's not that the Royal Marines can't or won't undertake opposed landings, but they point out that such landings have always had the least chance of success, and obviously result in great and sometimes unacceptable casualties to one's own side. The object of war is, after all, to win and not simply to look good on the newsreels or provide the inspiration for a thousand books, plays, poems and films. But an unopposed landing demands speed, mobility and surprise (commando attributes all) and this is one reason why Royal Marine landing craft, while offering less physical protection than their US counterparts, are quicker; why the Royal Marines are trained to land in spots previously regarded as being inaccessible; and why they're also trained to land and fight in small units, only linking up later in larger formations if necessary. The other reason is that the US equipment is extremely expensive. As a colonel in the US Army once remarked, if Britain had had the same amount of money to spend on arms as the Americans had, her troops would not be as well trained as they are today. In British forces, training and tactics have had to make up for budgetary shortfalls – which is no very bad thing, since it produces soldiers less dependent on high-tech equipment that invariably breaks down just when it's most needed. As can be imagined, this amphibious ability of the Royal Marines demands very high standards of landing-craft officers and NCOs, and Poole is where they're trained.

The Royal Marines use five types of craft for their amphibious operations; in descending order of size they are:

Land Craft Utility (LCU) The latest LCU, model 9R, in service since 1987, carries 120 men plus kit or up to 70 tons of stores at a speed of 9 knots (11 m.p.h.) with a maximum of 600 nautical miles. It boasts its own small crane and the cargo area can be totally or in part weatherproofed for operations in the Arctic. The crew of 6 have their own basic (very basic) accommodation which includes a small galley.

Landing Craft Vehicle and Personnel (LCVP) This has a top speed of around 18 knots (21 m.p.h.) and can carry 35 men plus kit or, say, a LandRover plus trailer. It can also be weatherproofed for arctic operations, and will have a maximum crew of 3.

Rigid Inflatable Boats (RIBs) Similar in design to the fast inshore boats used by the Lifeboat Services. An RIB can carry up to 10 men and their kit and will reach a speed of 45 knots (50 m.p.h.) RIBs are used in Hong Kong by 3 Raiding Squadron RM in their anti-smuggling duties.

The major task of 3 Raiding Squadron used to be intercepting refugees from mainland China and Vietnam before they could land in the colony and disappear from sight – usually to be exploited by unscrupulous employers. But of late, the squadron's tasks have enlarged to prevent the smuggling – in or out of the colony – of drugs, gold and even pornography. The Royal Marines fulfil a similar customs function on the island of Diego Garcia in the Indian Ocean, also using RIBs, since although a US base, Diego Garcia remains Crown property.

Norway – a Rigid Raider and LCVP move out to sea. The LCVP has been covered ('Arcticized') to protect Marines from the sub-zero temperatures in ship to shore transit. (Inset) Wearing the cap comforters that mark them as the King's Squad, recruits in an LCVP off Devon. In the foreground, two King's Badge candidates, shown by the red diamonds worn on the left arm

Rigid Raiders (known in the Corps simply as Raiders) can carry 5 men in arctic kit and 6 men in tropical or temperate kit for up to 50 nautical miles at a speed of 30 knots (36 m.p.h.) At present the Corps is looking to replace the current model by one with a slightly larger payload, but the basic design won't change very much.

Gemini inflatables are also used, but more in a special forces role, e.g. in delivering the SBS to a point on land or at sea, and then picking them up again. Geminis are more likely to be used in submarine-based operations, since their size and total collapsibility make for easy storage.

Because of their greater size, LCUs can and do become 'mother' ships for an amphibious operation, allowing the infinitely larger LPDs (Landing Platform Dock, e.g. HMS *Fearless* or *Intrepid*) to slope off into the wide blue sea where they'll run less risk of being attacked by enemy aircraft or submarines. LCVPs may also be used as temporary HQs, as well as mounting diversionary or surprise attacks in areas other than the main landing beach. And, if radio silence is being rigorously enforced, Raiders can and do act as high-speed couriers between the various elements of the amphibious landing force. During the Falklands, LCVPs were also used as inshore minesweepers. Much to their own and everyone else's relief, it transpired that no mines were actually in the area around San Carlos, but it did demonstrate the versatility of these craft, and indeed of the landing-craft branch as a whole.

Not only is the Landing Craft Company at Poole responsible for training men in the branch, it also trains all Royal Marines how to function in landing craft. It is possibly here that a Royal Marine begins to develop, for the first time, that sense of caution that is very much the Corps' own trademark. It is impossible to spend any time in or around the sea without learning to expect the worst as a matter of course. (The worst, in the case of a recruit practising landing drills for the first time, is discovering that the coxswain of an LCVP has not dropped the ramp on to a gently shelving beach. He's dropped it on a sand bar some distance offshore and the recruit has to wade ashore, rifle held high, in water that comes just under his chin.)

539 reborn

One can't talk about landing craft without also mentioning 539 Assault Squadron RM, even though they're based at Plymouth and not Poole. 539 is the unit mainly responsible for carrying out infiltration and flanking attacks, using LCUs, LCVPs, Rigid Raiders and Inflatable Raiding Craft (IRC – Geminis). First formed during the Falklands War, 539 was disbanded soon after victory, only to be re-formed in 1984 – thus carrying on the Corps tradition of forming, disbanding and then re-forming units again and again until the powers that be give up the struggle and allow the Corps to do what it wanted in the first place.

One of 539's more spectacular techniques is one whereby a Raider is lifted from the sea by helicopter and transported up the coast or inland to a river, fjord or lake so that amphibious attacks can take place where they're least expected. None the less, 539's primary role is still a subject for much discussion, not to mention heated argument. Is it primarily concerned with special forces operations or even simply conventional operations, or is

Somewhere off Gibraltar, 42 Commando's Recce Troop practise covert insertion techniques from a hunter/killer submarine of the P&O (Porpoise and Oberon) class. A technique used by the SBS to recce the Falklands while the main Task Force was still at Ascension Island

its main task the movement of men and stores to the beachhead – i.e., is 539 tactical or logistical? The 539 would probably say that it will go where it's most needed, but will also point out that the ability to mount flanking, infiltration and diversionary attacks allows the Royal Marines far greater flexibility. In practice, in war 539 becomes one of those assets that belong to the commander who can make the best case for using them.

Marine Drivers

The other major training responsibility at Poole is for Royal Marine Drivers. Driving is never seen as being one of the more glamorous tasks in any armed force. The general impression is usually of a surly, dirty driver managing to hide both himself and his vehicle with practised ease. That may have been good forty years ago but military drivers nowadays must be more skilled and responsible, particularly Marine drivers. Think about it for a moment. Before a truck or Land-Rover can be driven off a landing craft, its engine must be waterproofed, since it may well be under water for some considerable period of time. It must be waterproofed in such a way that the vehicle doesn't have to be stripped down immediately, as in the old days, as soon as it reaches dry land, in order to remove all the waterproofing. Nowadays, a Land-Rover or three-tonner, when waterproofed by the Marines, can be driven for the next six months or so. It doesn't do the vehicle a power of good, but it does save time. That waterproofing is the responsibility of the drivers themselves, who have to know how to keep their vehicles moving when *they're* one hundred per cent submerged for well over a minute, being guided by a man standing behind them with his head just above the surface.

They also have to know how to make the BVs (bandwagons, tracked vehicles used on snow and ice) perform to a level that the manufacturers never intended. Sometimes it feels as if a good driver can make a BV walk on tiptoe through an icefield. Of course he can't, but the skill with which he moves the BV across the most dangerous terrain is something to experience – to experience with a certain amount of alarm, actually, until one discovers how far a BV can lean to one side without overbalancing.

There's one aspect of the Marine Drivers Branch that, again, epitomizes the Corps' penchant for perfecting a particular military skill to the point where they become *the* experts. Poole teaches the VIP staff drivers, who learn anti-terrorist techniques, taught to a standard considerably higher, say, than that of the civilian police. The Marines teach not only how to use the car as a weapon in case of ambush, but also how to execute particularly snappy U- or J-turns, and how to do so without becoming disoriented, so that the driver can immediately and accurately fire his weapon after the car has come to a shuddering halt or crash. In other words, weapon training is as much a part of the VIP staff driver's course as driving itself.

Yet with all that, the Drivers Branch never has enough volunteers. Traditionally, a Marine Driver used to be a man in his mid to late thirties who'd grown a little tired of all the yomping that's done by a rifleman. And who, wanting to gain some skill for later civilian life, became a Driver – knowing that he'd be trained on, and licensed to drive, very large trucks. Unfortunately, there aren't as many 'three-badge' Marines around as there used to be. Not only that, but the demand for Drivers increases yearly, resulting in it often being 'suggested' to a young Marine that being a Driver is exactly what he wants to do. Sometimes it is; more often it isn't, and that means that many Marines leave the Corps earlier than they'd intended because they haven't had the opportunity to do the job they wanted. It has been argued that those men to whom driving is 'suggested' would be better off in that branch than in a commando unit anyway, for whatever reason; and that, ultimately, Corps needs must take precedence over individual ambitions. From personal observation, most young Drivers are more than capable of being a rifleman within a commando unit – indeed if they're not, then there's something wrong with recruit selection and training. (This does highlight the fact that often the Corps'

539 Squadron. With his number two being winched into the Sea King, the coxswain secures the outboard motor. Already the Rigid Raider has cleared the waves and the helicopter has begun to move forward

overall man management leaves a little to be desired.) In drafting men as Drivers – not exactly against their will, but having given them a single choice of career option – the Corps is only treating the symptoms (lack of Drivers) rather than the disease (lack of volunteers). In fact, it's very much a Royal Naval solution to a manpower problem – simply to draft men into a particular branch that's understaffed. But then, as they say, if a man can't take a joke, he shouldn't have joined the Corps in the first place.

The display team

Poole also contains R Company, which is the public face of the Royal Marines. It is R Company which tours Britain giving various displays – unarmed combat apparently the favourite. Between April and September the commando display team will give 90 exhibitions to over 1.5 million people. And as part of the display team, the Royal Marines free-fall team gives 140 displays. All this is great fun, and it's nice for the taxpayer to see where his or her money is going to, but that's not the only reason for R Company's existence. It is an extremely effective recruiting method. It's not that they seek to impress the embryonic killers amongst us – that type of person is unlikely ever to be considered for the Corps, and if they were, wouldn't make it through training without being found out and thrown out. What R Company does extremely effectively is get across the Corps' commitment to excellence within a military context. If you could examine the earlier lives of all those young men who joined the Marines without being able to give any specific reason – other than their own belief that the Marines are an elite, the best, and represent something special – you'd probably find that the recruit or YO had seen a Royal Marine display team when he was a boy, and somehow the memory had stuck. This fact is well understood by one or two left-wing councils who refuse to allow the display team anywhere near the schools in their area.

Trials Unit

Hidden away amongst RM Poole's complex of offices and lecture halls is a Trials Unit, specializing in researching, developing and sourcing equipment that will be used mainly by the Special Boat Service. Equipment can range from rucksacks to boots to diving gear to weapons to UHF burst transmitters, with built-in encrypt and scrambler facilities. But although mainly involved with the SBS, much of the Trial Unit's knowledge and experience will filter down to a rifleman in a commando – from the SBS to the recce troop (at commando level) and from there to the companies and troops themselves. And while the SAS also trial their own equipment, because the SAS is further removed from the rest of the army – with the exception of the Parachute Regiment – much of the SAS expertise and knowledge takes much longer to filter down, if it ever does.

The SBS, being an integral part of the Royal Marines, find it easier to pass on their knowledge. Much of the equipment that a Marine buys for himself (boots, knives, compasses even) is selected because of the SBS experience, or that of the M&AW Cadre who also trial equipment.

Finally, the SBS also train at Poole and are discussed in the next chapter, as are the M&AW Cadre (MLs Branch) and Comacchio Group. The SBS and ML branches are open to both officers and men.

6/SBS AND THE CADRE

Cadre member climbing on
Dewerstone and (opposite)
10,000 feet high, at 40 degrees
below zero Fahrenheit, the
Cadre on patrol in Norway

To many, the men of the Special Boat Service and the Mountain and Arctic Warfare Cadre epitomize the spirit and ability of the Royal Marines. Who are these men, and how do they train? What is their use in conventional warfare? And how did Comacchio Group, Royal Marines, become one of the most effective anti-terrorist organizations in the British Armed Forces?

Special Boat Service

The motto of the Special Boat Service is 'Not by Strength [but] by Guile'. As one of their major conventional roles is beach reconnaissance, they can achieve their objectives more easily by being more thoughtful, by relying on their imagination and intellect than by storming in guns blazing. Indeed, they are trained to apply the same principles when they act in a more active role – a 'softly, softly catchee monkey' approach permeates their entire training programme, plus a dedicated professionalism.

The SBS is officially described as being the Royal Navy's own special forces. For that reason, only Royal Marines and Royal Navy personnel are eligible to join, with the vast majority of personnel coming from the Marines. They work closely with the SAS (which is known as Supply and Stores or 'them up the road' – Hereford being further north than Poole – as much for security reasons as anything else). In fact, the SBS are extremely security conscious, which they justify on several grounds.

First, a good deal of their work, even in a conventional role, involves the use of classified equipment. Not only that, but the more specialized and vital the role undertaken by any unit, invariably the narrower comes the division between success and failure. Allowing an enemy, or potential enemy, to know in advance the operational and tactical methods used by the SBS is more likely to doom any mission in the conventional role to failure. It makes little sense to admit what one's capabilities are – far better that they should come as an unpleasant surprise.

Second, in their anti-terrorist role, the same applies but to a far greater extent. With their responsibility to counter any terrorist action at sea, the SBS are far more vulnerable than the SAS in many of their operations, since the SBS have far fewer options open to them in getting to their objectives – they can't blast in through a wall, swing in through a window or parachute on board without being seen. And once having got on to a hijacked oil rig or ship, it is far harder to make it secure because of the very size and complexity of its internal structure, not to mention the number of people on board.

Previous pages: A Cadre four-man recce team on covert insertion. Flotation achieved by waterproof 'bivvy bags' or sleeping bag covers

Opposite: An SBS pre-selection course. With only six hours sleep in the previous three days, the candidates had been sent on a timed twenty-mile yomp. At halfway they were faced with an unexpected river crossing (note the strapping on the men's bodies used to prevent chafing from their equipment and 50-pound bergens). Those that finished the twenty-miler had to spend the night outside, each man on his own, in just the clothes he stood in. Followed the next day by a timed thirty-mile yomp, which finished with a quarter-mile swim out to sea to a waiting LCU. And all this in only the first few days of the two-week pre-selection course. But already the instructors have 'pinged' those they want to make it – the kind of man who 'would crawl fifty miles on his knees to make an RV (rendezvous)' – men in the SBS must have total confidence in each other

As a member of an anti-terrorist unit, a man in the SBS is a possible target for foreign intelligence organizations plus terrorist groups themselves. Hence comes their blanket refusal to allow individual members to be identified. Not even with slightly coy bars across their faces can serving members of the SBS appear in photographs, and their names may not be published.

Third, the SBS are aware that the publicity that the SAS 'enjoy' often works against that organization, and that the SAS spend a good deal of their time denying that they were ever anywhere near a particular incident when it took place, and that they've found it a little harder to do their job effectively within the media gaze.

In terms of the common good, it seems that a line must be drawn on occasions between the public's right to know and the public's need to know – and, indeed, between a newspaper's need to sell more copies.

However, the secrecy surrounding the SBS may also work against them, since it's resulted in a superman image, even amongst serving Royal Marines, and that in turn affects recruiting to the branch. Many Marines feel that as much as they'd like to join the SBS, they're not up to the pre-selection course, let alone the training itself. However, the pre-selection course is, the SBS firmly states, based on the level of fitness of the average Royal Marine in a fighting company. Which is to say, very fit indeed compared to civilian life, but not unduly so in a military environment. As for the course itself, anyone taking it does get fitter as time goes on. Fitness, however, is not all, and the mental attributes needed to pass pre-selection and training should not be ignored.

Pre-selection lasts for two weeks. Each man is obviously a volunteer, as with the SAS. But whereas any man in the Army – or British armed forces – can volunteer to join the SAS and, within reason, must be allowed to try, volunteers for the SBS must be recommended by their units. Unless a man is as fit as someone in a rifle troop, has a proven will to succeed and is at home on or in the water, he won't be recommended. Simply because he won't pass.

The essence of the pre-selection course is that none of the candidates have the faintest idea what's going to happen next. They know that they'll be in the diving-aptitude phase, but not what that means. They may have talked about the pre-selection course with another Marine who tried but failed – but the instructors vary it enough so that the elements still come as a surprise. Most of the pre-selection will be done with fifty-five-pound bergens on the men's backs. So far so good, because in a rifle troop a man will be used to carrying up to twice that amount on exercise. But not night and day. Not when running, as opposed to marching or skiing. Not day after day after day – as well as night after night, because the candidates don't get all that much sleep.

At some point, following a modest twenty-mile yomp, the candidates may be loaded into the back of a three-tonner and told to snuggle into their sleeping bags and get their heads down for the rest of the night. Sure enough, as soon as they're asleep they're woken up – if they've managed to get any sleep, because the three-tonner will have driven at breakneck speed over the roughest ground it can safely cross – and made to get out of the (stationary) three-tonner, stripped, given a little PT and then stood to

attention while someone with a 'loud, squeaky voice' harangues them – a very basic resistance-to-interrogation test. They're then given back a bare minimum of clothes and told to make themselves comfortable for the rest of the night – but not together. Each man is given his own area in which he must stay. What the instructors are looking for at this point is the men who've got the initiative and drive to burrow immediately beneath a bush or pile of leaves. Anybody who has to be told what to do is unlikely to pass. At some time after that – anything up to twenty-four hours – the men set off on a thirty-mile yomp, still carrying their bergens, which finishes with a longish swim out to an anchored ship.

At another stage of their training – and this at a time when they've had little or no sleep for three days and nights – the men will be taken into an overheated and badly ventilated classroom. There, they'll be shown a film that, in a 'boring film of the year' award, would win hands down. Imagine, if you will, a film about men loading different-coloured oil drums on to a truck. Loading, unloading and reloading them. Over and over again. Sometimes all the drums of one colour are loaded first. Sometimes drums of varying colours are loaded, often in different sequences. Sometimes all the men load the drums. Sometimes, only a few of them do. Imagine too, that you've had no sleep for well over forty-eight hours. That the room you're in is extremely warm and stuffy. Imagine, too, that at the end of the film you're going to be tested on how the drums were loaded and who did the loading. How long could you stay awake?

It is an extremely good test of concentration, observation, stamina and desire to stay on the course. It emphasizes that intelligence-gathering for real usually takes place when the operative is exhausted, and in far from ideal conditions. Rumour has it that everyone falls asleep at some point during the film, and that the written answers to the questions are mere scrawls.

In many ways the diving-aptitude tests are the hardest for the SBS don't train to dive in the crystal-clear waters of TV documentary fame, but in cold, silt-clogged seas where a man can't see a hand in front of his face. They train to dive at night, making the darkness even more impenetrable. The reason for this is that since the Royal Marines and therefore the SBS have a responsibility for NATO's northern flank, i.e. Norway, training conditions should simulate as much as possible operational conditions – especially on the pre-selection beat-up. Then, too, the SBS must be able to leave or join a submerged submarine, utilizing a tiny, cramped escape chamber. The bottom line is that the SBS is no place for anyone who suffers from any form of claustrophobia. It is often the diving aspect more than any other that defeats men on the pre-selection – that and their mental attitude.

Even if a man does manage to last out the full two weeks without either leaving on his own accord or being binned (returned to his unit), it is no guarantee that he'll be passed for further training. All the instructors will have to decide if they want him back and the vote must be unanimous. A few of those who fail will, genuinely, be asked to try again later. But as it is, there is a less than thirty per cent pass rate on the pre-selection course, which the SBS find extremely frustrating. They're convinced that there are many Marines who could pass the course, who could become valued

Right: Checking the closed circuit breathing apparatus of a Dutch SBS team before an anti-ship hijacking op.
Below: Using 'jumars' or metal clamps, a Dutch SC moves up the side of the (hijacked) ship.
Far right: Two Dutch SCs effecting entry via the anchor chain and hawse hole. In real life, this type of operation would probably be done at night

Candidates for the Royal Marines SBS training on Klepper canoes. The front man steers by rudder bars, controlled by his feet

members of the service and who would enjoy being so, but who are put off trying for all the wrong reasons.

The reasons why a man joins the SBS are often as difficult to ascertain as why he joined the Corps in the first place. For some men it was because having worked with the SBS – say as a member of a recce troop – and learnt a bit about them and what their role was, joining the Service became the logical thing to do. For others, it was simply that they wanted to get to the top of their profession as Marines, and to them the SBS were – and are – the best. The SBS are, however, quick to deny any elitism on their part. They say that they are Marines first and foremost, that many of their close friends are in other branches, and each part of the Corps is as important in its own way as any other. For one member of the SBS, it was totally inconceivable that anyone would willingly fly helicopters at full speed only a few feet above ground. Another man made the point that his own life could just as easily depend on a driver being in the right place at the right time, or the coxswain of a Rigid Raider, or that if it weren't for the proficiency of the DL or PW Branches, there'd be no raw material for the Marines, let alone the SBS. Meaning that few men, if any, join the SBS because they see themselves as heroes, and the ones that stay are those who genuinely enjoy 'the job' for its own sake.

For the man who has passed the pre-selection, training begins with a fifteen week course – all good, embuggerance stuff designed to further test

his aptitude for what he'll be learning later. Assuming he passes that, he's then faced with a further eleven weeks of 'trade' training: specialized diving techniques; beach reconnaissance; signals including UHF morse transmitting and receiving; advanced weapon training; demolition and sabotage; anti-terrorist drills; parachuting into the Arctic ocean; canoeing and survival exercises. If he manages to pass, he then becomes an SC3 – Swimmer Canoeist Third Class. But he's still on probation for another eighteen months, during which time the service will get a good look at him on operations and decide if he's really going to be a useful member of the SBS. If he does pass the SC3 probationary period, he'll then be expected to take an SC2 course, after which he'll be eligible for promotion to corporal within the branch – assuming he also manages to pass his Junior Command Course back at Lympstone. Similarly, if he passes his SC1 course, he'll still have to pass the Senior Command Course at Lympstone before he'll be promoted to sergeant within the service. An interesting feature of the SC2 and SC1 courses is that for a lot of the time the candidates conduct the course themselves, lecturing the others about various subjects they've had to study up on, or have had personal experience of – but always under the instructors' watchful gaze.

There is no question that the SC3 course is one of the toughest in all the armed forces throughout the world – not so much for the physical aspect, but because of the mental demands it places on a man. One serving SBS Marine likened it to perpetually walking on the edge of a precipice. You could look down and see all those other men who'd given up and left the course – and very comfortable they looked too. You always knew how easy it was to go over the same edge – just one little step, and it would be all over. But you also knew that once you decided to wrap, that was it because there's no going back in mid air.

The same man also said that it was the little things that got to you during the SC3 course. For example he, being smaller and thinner than the average, tended to feel the cold more. And on those occasions when he was allowed the luxury of sleeping in a bed, he came to dread the moment he first put his feet on the cold floor in the morning; the act of getting out of bed became so hard there were many times he almost wrapped by simply staying where it was warm.

In a way that sums up the type of man the SBS look for. The man who can make that extra effort, day after day. The man who, if he's been caught out in a blizzard, say, and manages to get back to the safety of a tent, immediately sets about making himself a hot drink and puts on dry clothes rather than simply collapsing for a few minutes in a damp heap.

With all that, there has to be a sense of humour, a refusal to take oneself too seriously, however seriously you take the job. It's something that's common to both the SBS and SAS – as the US Special Forces discovered a few years ago when they attended the then Jungle Warfare School (JWS) in Johore Bahru, Malaya. The JWS was largely staffed by SBS and SAS personnel and – from the author's personal experience – one of their favourite 'bites' (otherwise known as mickey-taking) would be to begin a conversation about communism while everyone was sitting around a campfire. Gradually, the instructors would come to agree that there was probably a lot to communism, and wonder if perhaps they weren't all on the wrong side. And although the US Special Forces were usually sure they were being wound up, invariably they'd bite, begin long learned explanations as to how mistaken the instructors were – sometimes even showing a degree of shock and dismay. Except of course for those Americans who'd ever served with the Royal Marines and who could recognize a bite when they heard one. It's a strange sense of humour and in that instance underlines the fact that good special forces personnel feel no need to justify their existence – which is probably one more reason why the SBS dislikes publicity.

Comacchio Group

In January 1987 a convoy carrying nuclear depth charges ran off the road in a deserted part of Wiltshire. Only one newspaper managed to identify the Royal Marines guarding the convoy as coming from Comacchio Group – and even then, missed the implications of what they'd written.

For some years now, Comacchio Group's existence and role have been one of the more open secrets within the Marine Corps: nominally classified, but everyone knowing what their job was. Certainly it can be assumed that the Soviet Union knew what Comacchio Group's job was and is – otherwise they've wasted an awful lot of money hiring cottages around Arbroath and the Holy Loch for the GRU-tasked operatives (Soviet military intelligence).

Comacchio Company, as it was originally known (the name is from one of the Royal Marines' Second World War battle honours won in Italy) was first formed in 1981 in response to the threat posed to Britain's offshore oil installations by terrorist groups, who were becoming increasingly sophisticated in their operations and far less selective in their targets. The prospect of well-armed terrorists gaining control of a production platform and holding it, plus workers, to ransom – or simply blowing it up – was one that scared the hell out of European governments and the oil industry alike. It was impractical to station troops full time on the rigs themselves, because they would have to be special forces troops and there aren't enough to go around. None the less, it has been suggested that most major production platforms have at least one member of the SAS or SBS working on them at any one time, probably as roughnecks.

Since the Royal Marines, via the SBS, are responsible for counter-terrorist operations at sea, and since protecting the oil rigs was an obvious Royal Navy responsibility, it was decided to form Comacchio Company. This would contain men specially trained to recapture oil rigs, and would include members of the SBS and Royal Marine snipers. That was the beginning, and like Topsy (and so many other Royal Marine units or sub-units) Comacchio grew and grew – largely, it must be said, because Comacchio was extremely good at its job.

The Royal Marines have always had the responsibility of protecting the Royal Navy's nuclear assets in transit, and any country's nuclear assets are in transit far more often than is generally realized.

There's a popular misconception that once a nuclear device, always a nuclear device. The truth is that governments are understandably reluctant to let anyone else know the exact shelf life of a particular nuclear device – the time it can remain in service without being overhauled or

A member of Germany's GSG9 anti-terrorist group on operations with the Dutch Royal Marines. He's wearing body armour and carries the Heckler Koch MP5 sub-machine gun – used by both the SAS and SBS

replaced. Obviously the presence of fairly high levels of radiation will probably affect the electronics, if nothing else. So at regular intervals convoys will move nuclear devices for checking and maintenance. This poses a security problem, for guarding these convoys is not a job that can be privatized. It's not even a job that can be done by regular forces, since the threat comes not only from demonstrators – who could, unwittingly, cause the most horrendous accident – but from the more lunatic, or extreme, groups quite prepared to cause an accident if it will further their own political ends. In other words, troops are needed who have proved themselves to be particularly effective in counter-terrorist operations, and who have both the training and common sense not to over-react. Since the bulk of Britain's nuclear assets are assigned to the Royal Navy, the Royal Marines had, over the years, gradually taken on the job of protecting most if not all of them. And for once there had been very few dissenting voices from the other armed forces at the Corps taking on an exclusive role.

Initially, the job was done by a variety of Royal Marine sub-units, each taking it in turn to be on stand-by. They never knew when the call could come, since security was – and is – extremely tight. They would simply be given a few hours' notice to be at such and such a place, fully armed and equipped. As often as not they'd find themselves taking over convoy duties from another Royal Marines unit.

As time went on, it became obvious that a single unit should be tasked with nuclear convoy escort duty. As it was, the work had begun to interfere with 3 Commando Brigade's overall efficiency, since no one knew from one moment to the next which sub-unit would be called out and for how long. As Comacchio Company already had an anti-terrorist role, it seemed logical to combine the two functions.

Today, Comacchio Group is comprised of two companies.

O Company is responsible for oil-rig protection and certain other anti-terrorist functions, together with an SBS detachment.

P Company – or Penal Company as it's known – is responsible for nuclear convoy escort work, which it must be admitted does become a mite boring. But it can't be emphasized enough that P Company does not simply provide guards. That job could probably be done by the civilian police (who are involved anyway, if only because no member of the armed forces in this country can take action against a civilian unless he is requested to do so by a serving police officer) or by any infantry regiment. P Company's role is primarily anti-terrorist and they are not men to be messed about with. Whatever anyone thinks about the morality of nuclear weapons, the fact remains that they are dangerous even unarmed, and no one in their right mind should even think about disrupting a nuclear convoy. In time of war, or the build-up to war, P Company's role would increase in importance since they would then have to contend with Soviet Spetznaz troops, plus British fifth columnists and the more extreme anti-nuclear groups.

Comacchio Group, then, is the largest anti-terrorist force within Britain. Following a reorganization slated for August 1987, the operational HQ will probably move to Poole – certainly for maritime and anti-terrorist operations – to be run by the SBS itself.

Mountain and Arctic Warfare Cadre (M&AW Cadre)

Known within the Corps simply as 'the Cadre', the M&AW Cadre administers and trains Mountain Leaders. It also has an operational function, since the Cadre can and does fight as a unit. In war it is tasked by Brigade and above to provide long-range reconnaissance; to provide static OPs (observation posts) behind enemy lines; and to provide the occasional fighting patrol – as it did during the Falklands War when the Cadre took out members of the Argentinian 602 Group Special Forces who were holed up in Top Malo Farmhouse.

Mountain Leaders are the experts on mountain and arctic warfare, cliff assaults and survival techniques. Their job is to act as guides, advisors and teachers to the commando units, and they are found at every level from Commando HQ down to the troops. In particular, MLs will be found within Recce Troop – which will also often contain at least one SBS-trained Marine.

Mountain Leaders receive only half Special Forces pay. In many people's opinion this is slightly unfair since, while the SBS undoubtedly deserve their extra pay and allowances – particularly for diving – and while some members of the SAS are entitled to similar payments, because of the work *they* do, other SAS elements do approximately the same type of job as the Cadre, yet are paid more for it. And to be honest, the SAS Mountain Troop is not as skilled or as knowledgeable as the Cadre.

Like so many other skills within the corps, M&AW warfare is something the Marines quietly acquired over the years, often contrary to the then popular military wisdom. And when it finally became apparent that there was a real need for those skills, the Corps was ready and waiting in the wings to supply them. Originally, the ML Branch was known as the Cliff Assault Wing, and confined its expertise to getting troops off beaches. And although some members of the CAW were sent to improve

Demonstrating the speed needed for real-life ops, three Cadre members abseil simultaneously from a Lynx helicopter

their climbing techniques in Austria, Norway, Canada and the French Alps – and attended snow warfare courses in Scotland and Norway – the accent was still very much on cliff assaults from the beachhead. Once men plus equipment had managed to get up a cliff, the Cliff Leader's (CL) role diminished. But by the early 1960s, the CAW had become more and more involved in Cold Weather Warfare (CWW). By 1962 the CAW had changed its name to the Cliff Assault Troop (providing a permanent fighting nucleus), and had trained various companies from 43 Commando (now defunct) before they went to Norway on Exercise Donald Duck (12–24 October 1962). This exercise marked the beginning of 3 Commando Brigade's present responsibility (together with the Royal Netherlands Marine Corps) of protecting NATO's northern flank. Between 1962 and 1965 the Corps realized that helicopters would change the face of modern warfare. Increased troop mobility resulted in a greater need for accurate long-range reconnaissance. So in 1965 the Cliff Assault Troop were put through a reconnaissance course by the Platoon Weapons Branch at Lympstone, and subsequently renamed the Reconnaissance Leader (RL) Troop. RLs combined advanced climbing skills, cold-weather warfare skills and the reconnaissance skills of survival and sniping. At this time the Norwegians were regarded as being the experts on winter warfare. And yet the Corps found itself a little uneasy about the current Norwegian attitude to a possible Soviet/Warsaw Pact attack on northern Norway (strategically vital since whoever controls northern Norway effectively controls the North Atlantic). Discounting the possibility of battles being fought off the beaten track, the Norwegian plan was basically to guard the E9, the main road that runs the full length of the country. However, it's a foolish commander who plays into his opponent's strengths; Soviet commanders are far from foolish and the presence on the Kola Peninsula of large numbers of Mongolian-raised and trained troops suggested that Soviet plans called for a less simplistic approach. So it was that the Corps utilized the RL Troop to become *the* experts on mountain and arctic warfare – which they've done to such an extent that in 1986 the Norwegians requested their help in training Norway's own troops.

By 1970, the RL Troop had been renamed yet again, this time (finally?) as the Mountain and Arctic Warfare Cadre, and moved to its present location in Stonehouse Barracks, Plymouth.

(This whole process of naming and renaming conjures up a vision of an increasingly frustrated planner in the Ministry of Defence who discovers that every time he thinks he's managed to persuade the Royal Marines to give up one of their units he discovers, a few months or years later, that the unit continues to exist – but under another name.)

There is no ML3 rate within the branch, since it is primarily an instructor's branch, and all instructing in the Corps is done by corporals and above; corporals possess a 2 rating, so the Cadre trains only ML2s and ML1s. Officers take the ML2 course but not the ML1, since they don't have the time. Both courses last for nine months, and a good part of the ML1 course is spent instructing the ML2s.

Mountain Leaders must enjoy climbing. The Cadre will probably say no, climbing can be taught. As it can – but what can't be taught is an enthusiasm for mountains and for the wilderness. So while MLs don't need to be natural climbers in the sense of a Joe Brown, they do need to enjoy what they're doing. It's said that most MLs are failed SBS. The truth of the matter is that many MLs have tried for the SBS but were defeated by one thing – diving. Quite a few have even passed the pre-selection, only to decide that the prospect of doing the SBS type of diving did not please. Aside from that, both the Cadre and the SBS look for a similar type of man – self-confident, assured, professional and interested in the job for the job's sake, rather than any glory it may bring him.

Ordeal by ice

The following is a description of a day and a night on an ML2 course. It happened not so very long ago, when the trainees concerned were in the fifth month of the course and as close to exhaustion as it's safe to be in the Arctic.

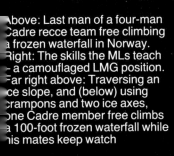

Above: Last man of a four-man
Cadre recce team free climbing
a frozen waterfall in Norway.
Right: The skills the MLs teach
— a camouflaged LMG position.
Far right above: Traversing an
ice slope, and (below) using
crampons and two ice axes,
one Cadre member free climbs
a 100-foot frozen waterfall while
his mates keep watch

The exhaustion showed when they packed up their tents one morning – a hard, frustrating business since frozen canvas is one of the most stubborn materials known to man. You could see the trainees check for a minute, summoning up the strength to kick the canvas into shape. You would see it in the way they packed up their gear to go climbing – trying so hard to summon up the will to concentrate on the job in hand. You could see it in the fixed determination on their faces to pass, to survive. A fit man is a relaxed man, and these men were too tired to allow themselves the luxury of relaxing for a single minute.

During the day the temperature had been a comfortable minus twenty degrees Fahrenheit. Comfortable, that is, as long as you stayed out of the shadows and the wind. But as the shadows lengthened and the wind freshened, the temperature plus wind-chill factor dropped to minus forty degrees Fahrenheit – cold enough to freeze bare flesh to metal instantly if anyone were foolish enough to work without gloves.

The ML2s were training at approximately ten thousand feet in the Norwegian mountains. The day had been spent practising the skills of ice climbing: how to use crampons and ice picks to claw one's way up sheet ice pitches; how to avoid grey or white ice as it's usually extremely brittle and will flake off in large chunks that will crash on to the man below. And learning that even blue or green ice, the hardest and most stable, will flake and splinter in the extreme cold.

One of the trainees had slipped on an ice pitch and cut his face open. Since wounds do not heal easily, if at all, in the extreme cold, he'd had to be taken back to base, some sixty kilometres away, hoping against hope that the injury would not prevent him from finishing the course. (Nor did it, and he eventually passed out near the top.)

But there was one particular trainee who was finding the going very difficult indeed. Harry (not his real name) had originally wanted to become an ML as much for a career move as anything else. It rather fitted in with his own image of himself, which was that of a supremely professional Royal Marine officer. And Harry was very conscious of being an officer. That in itself tends to be an un-officer characteristic, particularly amongst the young lieutenants in the Corps, and particularly on an ML course, where rank plays no part and has no privileges. Nor had Harry managed to develop that particular bloodymindedness that can help to counter a flawed motivation; nor did he appear to be totally at home in the mountains. To counter that, he had his pride, extreme physical fitness and possibly an overdeveloped sense of *noblesse oblige* – Harry was going to pass the ML2 course because officers couldn't fail.

But his fellow trainees had begun to doubt Harry's ability to pass; the instructors had certainly begun to doubt it; and in his heart of hearts, Harry himself had also begun to doubt his ability to pass. Unfortunately, his perceptions of how an officer should behave had prevented him from sharing his self-doubts with his fellow trainees, and even of examining them more closely himself. If only he had done so, he would – paradoxically – have found the course that much easier to take.

Generally speaking, there are two types of people who successfully complete special forces training. There are those who are the supreme naturals, who find it all quite easy. These men are few and far between.

M&AW CADRE – ML2 and ML1 TRAINING PROGRAMME

Month	ML2	ML1
September	Cornwall – climbing, including free climbing (without ropes) at night	Instructs ML2 course
October	Wales – climbing Isle of Islay – survival training (classified) – resistance to interrogation	Wales – upgrading own standards of climbing
November	Mountain training	Detached to Commando units for assessment as instructors
December	Mountain training and arctic techniques	Norway preparation
January	Norway – snow and ice techniques	Detached to Commando units as instructors
February	Norway – ski patrol and resistance to interrogation	Continuing instruction
March	Norway – final exercise	Rejoin ML2 course for exercise
April	Scotland – climb on Ben Nevis	Scotland – climb on Ben Nevis

Men on the ML1 course who are detached to units as instructors are continually assessed as to how good they are at instructing. It doesn't matter how good they are at the skills of their trade, they must also be able to teach those skills to other Marines of all ranks. They must also show a good deal of maturity since in the Arctic, the ML1 – and to a lesser extent the ML2 – is the man to whom everyone else looks for advice, from the CO of a commando on down.

Then there are the others who do find it difficult and are forced to dig deep within themselves for the motivation, the energy to carry on. In the process they are forced to become totally honest with themselves, and by extension, totally honest with each other.

It's often obvious when a man is going through this particular 'dark night of the soul', the time when he comes face to face with himself, with all his weaknesses as well as his strengths. The man becomes a little, often more than a little, introverted as he begins to strip away the barriers built up over the years. At some point he more or less has to make the decision – not whether to carry on, but whether he deserves to carry on. For some people this process is so alarming that they refuse to face it. Possibly there is some dread secret that they can't bear to confront.

The really 'special' thing about special forces personnel is that they have all passed through this process of self-knowledge and learnt to accept themselves as they really are.

But Harry had put off and put off his inner confrontation, still would not admit it openly when he couldn't cope. His clinging so desperately to a self-image born of less trying times had come close to having him thrown off the course. And as the pressure grew, Harry had begun to fall apart. His kit had become totally disorganized. His mess tins – always a good indication of a man's morale – had become filthy, encrusted with the remains of hastily snatched meals. If it hadn't been so cold, Harry would probably have gone down with food poisoning. He had, to an extent, become the butt of the other trainees' humour – yet the ML2 course is the last one in the world that needs a natural class clown.

Ice climbing over, trainees skied back down the valley to where a collection of ten-man conical tents had been pitched directly on to the hard-packed snow. That night the outside temperature was to go down to minus seventy degrees Fahrenheit – including the wind chill – which is cold enough to worry anyone, experiencing it for the first time, that they won't wake up in the morning. But warmed by the trainees and a solitary candle, the temperature inside the tents remained at a comfortable minus fifteen Fahrenheit.

The rule in the Arctic is that one should always be in a sleeping bag at night unless there's a guard duty or some other chore to be done. Men cook from their sleeping bags, repair and pack kit from their sleeping bags – and if they could, they'd urinate from their sleeping bags. As it is, the need to urinate invariably strikes at about 0300, and the tent becomes noisy with groans followed by curses as someone gets out of his nice, warm sleeping bag, gets dressed and makes his way outside into forty below.

All the trainees in Harry's tent had got into their bags as soon as possible. But Harry was still up, wrestling with a recalcitrant crampon. During the time he'd spent on it, the others had managed to cook themselves an evening meal, prepare a hot drink for the morning, shave, sort out their kit for the next day, and settle down for the night. And Harry still wrestled with his crampon.

It was a measure of the way the other trainees thought of him that no one had offered to help. For the rule is that one only helps a man who can help himself and help you in return. There is no way that the trainees will carry a man on the ML2 course – they haven't the energy and the instructors wouldn't let them. They would – and did – help Harry to the extent that they wouldn't let him die up there, but that's as far as it went. That meant the time was fast approaching when Harry might be faced with two choices: quit of his own accord, or be binned.

Interestingly enough, Marines appear to have more respect for a man who quits of his own accord, recognizing that he's just not up to it, than the man who's binned after it it's become apparent that he's not going to finish training. First, it does take a certain moral integrity to be able to face oneself and admit that you've failed – even though it may not be through any fault of your own. Secondly, the man who hangs on and hangs on is usually trying to get his fellow trainees to get him through, giving nothing in return. As we've seen, that's one of the unforgivable sins in the Corps.

Food cooked, every last bit of snow brushed from their sleeping bags (in case it melted, then froze later, forming a cold spot), gear ready for the next day, the trainees settled down for the night. All except Harry, who had only now begun to cook his food. And again tiredness told as he tried to take a short cut in lighting his cooker, the whole thing caught fire and burning fuel covered his hand. A chorus of 'Oh, Harry' was heard in the tent, followed by 'Get you and the effing stove outside before we all go up.'

'Knew you'd give your right arm for me, mate, but you don't have to *flambée* it!'

'Playing at Buddhist monks, Harry?'

Belize, dawn. One member of a two man SBS team makes his way to the waiting helicopter. Note the extra pouches on his webbing

Little harm had been done except to Harry's already damaged self-esteem. Finally, he managed to get to bed.

The next day, the trainees – after packing up their camp – were taken to learn how to traverse a snow slope, and how to use an overhanging snow cornice as a hidden observation post – not by peeping around the corner, but by burrowing inside it – something that requires a good deal of nerve, as well as skill.

Ahead of the trainees was the final exercise, 300 kilometres of escape and evasion finishing with a particularly brutal resistance-to-interrogation session. Somehow, Harry had still been there at the end, and was eventually given a provisional pass. This meant that he would effectively be on probation for the next eighteen months; if the Cadre felt that he wasn't up to the job, that his climbing techniques hadn't improved sufficiently, then his rate would be taken away from him. Or if that proved difficult, he would never serve in an operational role with the Cadre.

Below zero options

On the other hand, two men who had been at the top of the course were failed when the instructors discovered that they had slept overnight in one of the huts that dot the Norwegian mountains, totally against orders. The disappointment in the Cadre when the two men were discovered was real and perplexed. No one knew why they'd done it. The rules were that trainees stay tactical at all times, meaning snowholes and tents. The result was an instant binning. (On the bright side, one of the men applied again for an ML2 course the next year. At the latest sighting he was doing well again – and sticking to the rules.)

The Cadre also trains all British troops who have been given an arctic warfare role – those who go as garrison troops to the Falklands, or those whose turn it is to be part of the ACE Mobile Force, the NATO reinforcement unit slated to help the UK/NL Marines. Unfortunately, few of the British contingents are proving up to the job – largely because Mountain and Arctic Warfare is not something that can be taught in a single season, as the planners appear to expect. Given their choice, the Cadre and indeed the Royal Marines would far rather that the Parachute Regiment had been allowed to continue as an integral part of the ACE Mobile Force; as it is, the Fusiliers have now taken over, and while their role is not intended to be as specialized as that of the Royal Marines, it will take at least two more years before they can begin to be at all effective. This is as much a comment on conditions in Norway – legitimately described as amongst the worst in the world – as it is on the attitude (possibly commendable, but unfortunate) of many British armed units, who automatically assume that they can handle any conditions simply because they are professional.

But as a Guards unit recently discovered, this is not always the case. En route for a tour in the Falklands, they had shown little interest in the advice and training that members of the Cadre attempted to give them. It wasn't until they arrived at Port Stanley, in a white-out, and took over two hours to move themselves and their personal kit from the dockside half a mile up the road, that they realized how crippling cold-weather conditions can be.

7/DON'T PANIC

Lessons learnt by the SBS and M&AW Cadre are used in teaching Royal Marines how to survive in conditions that would probably kill a civilian. And while it's unlikely that any civilian would ever face those extreme conditions, it's worth considering that survival is very much a matter of state of mind – of common sense coupled with a degree of practical training

Survival

Military survival is very different to civilian survival.

Civilian survival is essentially a matter of staying alive until someone comes to rescue you. Or of making sure you can be seen easily by potential rescuers. Military survival teaches how to stay hidden until you can make your own way back to friendly troops. Or to man an OP without being seen. Either way, you do not want to attract attention to yourself. This means that the 'hunter and gatherer' role so beloved of various textbooks has little or no place in military survival – unless you're lost in peacetime, in which case the rules for civilian survival apply.

The first rule, in either case, is DON'T PANIC. It's not easy to say when you're stuck out in the middle of nowhere, with nothing to eat, and with maybe an injured companion to worry about – or even a broken bone in your own body. But panic saps energy and makes you do silly things. Panic also saps the will to survive. The next rule is to use your COMMON SENSE – and remember the difference between theory and practice. Or, as a Marine survival instructor said:

'I often wonder why people buy all those books about living off the land, or how to survive in the jungle. There's not one person I know who can tell what an edible plant looks like after only seeing a drawing or a picture – no matter how accurate it is. You have to be shown the plant, in the flesh as it were. There's no other way.'

It's a wonderful idea, that there's enough 'natural' food out there to support one – and it totally disregards the fact that all but the most primitive peoples are farmers and herders. Nor do the majority of those who survive purely by hunting and gathering live a particularly fulfilling life, even by their own standards. The small percentage who have managed to attain a reasonably comfortable way of life have usually done so by adding trading to their skills – that and by playing host to a seemingly inexhaustible supply of scientists, explorers and journalists, all of whom provide an extra source of revenue, medicines and transistor radios. None the less, the legend has grown up that survival in the wild is

Previous pages: The sleeping and living platform of a snow hole being used for a brew-up. Note the toe-covers on the men's boots, used to prevent heat loss

Opposite above: A Ravenscar Force 10 tent provides good protection – specially in freezing rain! Below: 'Cloggies' in an Arctic basha. Sloping roof reflects heat from cooker, which is supported on bear paw snow shoes. Note how Marine who's cooking holds his glove, and hasn't made the mistake of putting it on the ground

possible, and without using any of civilization's tools – like guns or even fish hooks. It's not. It's the quickest way to dying unnecessarily. Probably a painful death, too.

The third rule is TAKE STOCK OF YOUR SITUATION. Figure out your assets – including human assets. There does appear to be such a character as a born survivor; and this person should become leader. According to the Cadre, he will be a person with common sense, imagination and stubbornness – and one who's prepared to do anything at all to stay alive. Not baulking at cannibalism if that's what it takes.

The Corps doesn't actually teach the best way of cooking human flesh. (Similar to any kind of meat really, although it does tend to 'go off' in temperate climates sooner than, say, beef or goat.) What the Corps would do is to hold up as examples of the 'natural' survivor those men in the Andean plane crash who survived by eating the flesh of their dead comrades. Of those survivors, the man who finally struggled through to get help was such a one, and even those survivors who initially baulked at the idea were, eventually, saved by the practice of cannibalism.

Hunting for your own food is, of course, a happier alternative, but unfortunately takes time and energy. And if it takes more energy to actually catch, say, a rabbit (high in protein, low in carbohydrate – not to be recommended as an exclusive diet) than you will get from *eating* it, the exercise becomes rather pointless. Similarly, while there are many edible plants around, it often does take an inordinate amount of time (and energy) to gather them. For example, nettles (boiled or dried and used as tea) may be one of the commonest plants in most parts of the country, but they seem to vanish in the more isolated areas. Fat hen, a plant that enjoyed a wide amount of publicity a year or so ago, is extremely difficult to identify. It also prefers growing close to civilization, which is irritating for potential survivors. Rosehips are a valuable source of vitamin C. But they're usually found in hedgerows, not in the wilds of Scotland. Certainly not in the Arctic during winter. Fungi may abound – but their season is fairly limited. They can also be pretty damn dangerous – and it only takes a fraction of the more virulent varieties to kill.

The Corps teaches a number of ways of testing wild plants. You can take a small amount – a very small amount – of the plant and put it between your front gums and lips. Leave it there for at least an hour, trying not to swallow too much, and if there's no stinging, or blistering, then you can reasonably assume that the plant is okay to eat. Quite how nutritious it'll be is another matter. Or you can crush a leaf or a stalk and tape it to a sensitive part of the body, say inside the armpit or in the crook of the elbow. Again, if after some time (at least twelve hours for this method) there are no unpleasant side effects, then you can be reasonably happy about eating it.

One of the Royal Marine survival experts was happy to explode a few myths:

'You know all those Japanese survivors left over from the last war that kept on being discovered in the jungles of Borneo or the Philippines? Guys who were doing their duty to the Emperor by staying alive and hidden from the enemy, who hadn't realized the war was over? Well, the papers made a big thing about how those guys had survived for so long in the ulu

[jungle]. But in every case it turned out that they'd survived largely by scavenging from isolated villages, or from abandoned slash-and-burn plantations. No way could they, did they, live off the land as I understand the term.

'By and large, the only people who can truly live off the land are the people who were born to do it. Have you ever examined the upbringing of a Bushman, say? You'll find that his first twelve or thirteen years are mainly devoted to learning just how to survive, and the process carries on throughout the rest of his short life. Now, he's got a natural aptitude for it – certainly he's born acclimatized – and he's surrounded by teachers, got nothing else to do with his time. But it does take a hell of a long time to learn those skills – and even with the Bushmen there are some guys who are never as good as the rest.

'Same goes for the Innuit [Eskimos] – and you don't find many of them using only harpoons these days. It's all rifles and snowmobiles. Again, the majority of so-called primitive tribes survive by a mixture of hunting, gathering and primitive farming – usually slash and burn. Where the hell the public gets the idea that anyone can learn, in a matter of months, to be able to survive totally unaided in the wild, any wild, beats me. They must have been reading too many books about it.'

It's unlikely that the average reader will ever have to survive in the Arctic, desert or jungle, it's unlikely that the average reader *could* survive in those areas for any great length of time – and certainly not on the basis of having read a few books on the subject. But every year, people are caught out in *temperate* wildernesses; some of them die because they don't know the basic rules of survival. Here, then, is an example of how you can survive if you followed Royal Marines teaching – with the proviso that most survival techniques are standard throughout the British armed forces.

The scenario is that you and three other civilians have been shipwrecked somewhere on the Scottish east coast. Two of your companions are injured – one with a broken leg, the other with possible broken ribs. Nothing of any note has been saved from the shipwreck. It's late autumn and the weather is atrocious – almost continual rain, often gale-force winds. The area you're in is totally deserted. There are signs that an attempt has been made recently to develop it for forestry, but those workers are long gone. You have found a single track that leads into the mainland – but you can see that it passes over the mountains that stand between you and the nearest settlement some forty or fifty miles away. You have only one set of oilskins between the four of you – and even if you had wanted to follow the track inland, early snow on the mountains has made you think twice. The most sensible course appears to be to wait where you are until you can attract the attention of a passing ship. But as few ships sail in those waters, and you won't be reported missing for at least another ten days, you have to be prepared for a long wait. What happens next? (This scenario is similar to one given Royal Marine officer candidates at a recent Admiralty Interview Board. Not many of them got it right, either.)

What doesn't happen is that one of the two fit people immediately sets off up the track on a rescue mission. The nearest main road is at least two days' walking away and will probably mean spending a night in the open. And unless you've been lucky enough to be shipwrecked with a mountaineer – or a serviceman who knows what he's talking about – the chances are that a walker won't make it.

More to the point, in order to make it, given the weather conditions, the walker will have to take the only set of oilskins. Whoever is left to look after the injured will spend all their time soaking wet. If an attempt is to be made, better to wait for a break in the weather – and better to be a little more prepared than you are at the moment.

The first thing you do is to move the injured people into the shelter of the trees – get off the beach as quickly as possible because beaches are rocky and slippery and if you're not careful, you'll end up with another broken leg. Once under the trees, you roughly splint the broken leg – making sure than the splint ties are not so tight as to restrict circulation, so causing gangrene, and you tape the suspected broken ribs as lightly as possible, using torn strips of cloth from the victim's own clothing. Don't use panty hose, because that can stretch or chafe. Besides, panty hose can be used as a water filter, a fish trap, string or simply to keep someone warm.

N.B. *Everyone who takes part in some form of outdoor activity should know basic first aid.*

Casualties reasonably well bandaged, your next problem is to keep them comparatively warm and dry while the two fit members of the party build a more permanent home. Dig down into the forest floor. Chances are that under several inches, even a foot or so, of leaves and pine needles you'll find that it's reasonably dry. Scrape out a depression, and line it with any dry foliage you can find. If necessary, tear a few live branches off the trees and beat them against a tree trunk to get rid of most of the moisture. Line the scrape with them, pile on a layer of dry – or dryish – pine needles, lay the injured on that and cover them in turn with more dry(ish) branches, pine needles and leaves. You can finish off the sandwich with wet leaves, as these will, to some extent, insulate the casualties. Now to look for a more permanent home. (You have, incidentally, got one working cigarette lighter with you. Which is just as well because without it you would be in very serious trouble indeed. Always carry a lighter or waterproof matches on your person when you are walking in the wild – or sailing inshore.)

The site of your home is going to be determined by a number of factors: proximity to a water supply; proximity to firewood; proximity to the beach – your most obvious source of food; and somewhere which allows easy access. Don't choose a cave high on a hill, because someone's bound to fall down it at night and you'll have three casualties on your hands.

So you look for and find a stream running down to the beach, through the forest – and through a part of the forest where there are many fallen branches. You also find a deadfall – a tree blown down by the wind with its top caught in the lower branches of another tree. It's ideal, because it's lying on a north-south axis and the prevailing wind is coming from the west. You now scavenge, remembering that there are signs that foresters or loggers have been in that location fairly recently.

Nature lovers the world over bemoan the fact that plastic and corrugated iron turn up in the most surprising places. Remember that and

begin to look for them. (Plastic and metal, not nature lovers!) They'll help save your life. You're out of luck with the corrugated iron, but you do find a couple of discarded plastic sacks and some thin-gauge plastic sheeting. Fine – the sacks will make sets of waterproofs, the sheeting insulation for your new home.

Stripping away the downside branches of the deadfall, you produce a very basic tent shape. Again, you scrape out a depression on the floor, trying to slope the sides gently down to a central point. Here you dig a hole two feet deep and measuring about six inches across, which you fill with stones. *Voilà*, one drain pit. You then fill the depression with more dry(ish) branches and leaves, remembering that you're going to have to sleep on it. Drape some of the plastic sheeting over the deadfall, sandwiching it between layers of more branches and leaves. Top the whole thing off with earth and grass taken from the sides of the stream – not too soggy, but damp enough to bond to the rest of the construction. The rest of the sheeting is hung up inside the shelter so that all the water on it can drain off. Do not put it on to the ground yet.

Now for the fire. Build a raised fireplace, or fire base, with stones. Shelter it from the prevailing wind with more stones. Don't build it inside the shelter, otherwise you'll smoke yourselves out. Try to give it as much protection from the rain as possible – make it its own little tent if necessary from large branches – and build a wall around it with more branches, small logs, etc., closed on all sides except the one facing the shelter entrance. This will reflect the heat into the shelter once the fire has

Demo brushwood basha with wooden heat reflector and (below) Arctic basha made from tent sheets plus two types of Arctic camouflage netting

started. Remember to leave a space on two sides of the fire base for drying out firewood. Now light your fire.

You can always find dry tinder *somewhere* in a forest. You might have to dig for it, you might have to break up rotten trees for it, but find it you can. Kindling you can usually get from the dead lower branches of trees, particularly conifers. The most important thing is to get a big blaze going as soon as you can – aside from the physical advantages of keeping you all warm and drying out clothes, it has a great psychological boost. Once it's going well, you can think about bringing the casualties to the shelter.

Incidentally, the casualties will not have spent the past few hours lying totally alone and wondering what the hell's going on. If they haven't been in a position to see what progress you've been making, you will have taken the time to check on them and give them a progress report – loss of morale will kill them more quickly than their injuries. So when you do bring them to the shelter – waterproofed and with a fire blazing – it'll be a tremendous boost. Arrange them as comfortably as possible in the shelter entrance – don't touch the spare sheeting yet – and consider the next stage. The first thing is to dry as much clothing as possible – but don't you, the fit ones, hang around the camp site while you're doing so. Get used to the idea that you're going to spend a large part of the time feeling damp and miserable. The important thing is to have warm clothes to sleep in. So take off most of your clothes and arrange them to dry in front of the fire – make this the responsibility of the injured. Again, injured people should always be given some task to do. It helps boost their morale as well as taking some of the load off your own back. You now make holes in the sacks for your head and arms (using your teeth if you don't have a knife, since teeth are more capable of precise work than a blunt stick or jagged stone) and set off on more foraging. Check out the stream – work your way upstream for at least a hundred yards to make sure that there are no dead sheep in it. The basic rule is that you should not take water from a stream within at least a hundred yards in either direction of a dead animal, and even then you're running a major risk. If there is an animal there, and you can't safely get water from higher up, move the carcass out – using sticks, not your hands. And then, at least a hundred yards up or down stream, dig a hole some three or more feet from the river bank, the bottom three feet below the stream level. Line it with charcoal taken from the fire. The water you finally get from this mini-well won't taste particularly pure, but it will have been filtered.

Even if there is no dead animal in sight, always make sure that you take water from the fast-moving part of the stream – where the water bubbles as it moves over the little rapids. Don't drink from the deeper and more still pools.

Next you'll need some sort of water container. Well, you're lucky enough to have an extra plastic sack. Failing that, you could make one out of plastic sheeting – a circular piece can obviously be made into a hollow cone. But you must wash the sack or sheeting first as it could have contained insecticide or fertilizer, either of which can harm you. The same applies to the sacks you're wearing.

If you don't have the plastic for a water container make one out of bark and mud or clay. Don't worry what it looks like, and don't worry if it falls to pieces after a few goes. You can always make another one – it's something else the casualties can do.

By now you've earned a hot drink. You take the filled container back to the camp site. The fire's blazing merrily – and you feel thankful that you had the foresight to put several loose stones between the fire and its base. By now, they've become red hot. You're also glad that you had the foresight to gather a few nettles, which you found in a sheltered part of the stream bank. These have been dried over the fire to the point that they crumble to the touch. The stones are placed as gently as possible into the container and naturally the water begins to heat up. You put the stones in one at a time, taking each one out as soon as it's transferred its heat to the water. Natually, you'll have chosen stones that are easy to pick up using two pieces of stick as tongs. If you don't take the stones out, chances are that their weight will break your container. Certainly by the time the water boils, you'll have more stones than liquid. As the water begins to warm up, crumble the dried nettle leaves into it – you'll need a biggish handful for the four of you. Alternatively, you can boil up fresh nettles, eat them and drink the liquid.

However, man cannot live on nettle tea or nettle soup alone. Nor, with the sea so close, will you need to. Limpets scraped or smashed from the rocks can be boiled or eaten raw. When the tide goes out, search rock pools for tiny crabs and shrimps – if nothing else, they'll flavour the nettle soup. There are all sorts of edible shellfish available – any doubts, and apply the taste test (a small bit held between the front gum and lower lip for an hour or so – no blistering or stinging, and it's reasonably safe to eat).

Aside from the seashore, in the ground, you've got worms. The preferred Royal Marine way of eating a worm is to first dip it into a glass of good brandy. Assuming that you don't have one, dry them out over the fire first and then add them to your soup.

And then there may be fish in the stream. Don't waste your time trying to fashion fish hooks or fish spears out of wood or thorns. You haven't got the time or the skill. What you should have done is fashion a basic stone knife by chipping an edge on it, much as your ancestors once did. Failing that, look for broken glass washed up on the shore, or razor shells. You should also check the shore for bits of nylon netting, plastic containers and driftwood.

Armed with some sort of knife, you move to the stream. Try to pick an area where fast-moving rapids empty into a fairly shallow broad area. If you've found some nylon netting, fix it across the stream at the downstream end of the still water, making sure the base is anchored firmly to the bottom. The top should be clear of the water level. If you couldn't find any nylon netting, you've got a little bit of construction work to do. Dam the area of the rapids – not completely, but enough to restrict the water flow by at least eighty per cent. Dig out the bottom of the stream so that there's a clear channel running downstream. Then you wedge branches at the furthest end of the channel so that the water can get out but nothing else. Or build a loose dam across the stream, with small spaces for the water to escape. Now go upstream beyond the first dam and move towards it, in the water, making as much noise and movement as you can. The idea is to drive the fish before you, to channel them into the current caused by the small gap in the first dam. (Ideally, that gap should result in a small waterfall so that the fish find it difficult to get back upstream.) Work the same stretch of water at least half a dozen times – starting a little higher up on each new approach. Finally, plug the gap in the first dam. The water in the stream below should now drain away through the channel you've dug. And if there are any fish there, they'll either be stranded on the bottom, or caught against the net if you had one. But do search the bottom of the stream very carefully – some fish will burrow into the mud, others will hide under stones. Fresh-water crayfish are fine to eat, but it's best to stay away from fresh-water mussels.

Small fish can be cooked whole – just be sure to cut off the fins and tail. A larger fish can be killed quite easily by simply putting your finger – or two fingers – into its mouth and jerking its head back, so breaking its neck. Cut off the head, fins and tail – these can be used for soup, but don't eat them: too bony. Now you can either scale the fish or not – if you haven't scaled it, you can't eat the skin. Cleaning it's no problem – a quick cut along the bottom of the body, running from the anal opening to the gills, and scoop out the contents. Your fish can now be grilled or wrapped in damp leaves and mud and baked in the fire embers. Or it can be boiled in the ubiquitous nettle soup – but first it should be wrapped in a piece of cloth. When it's done, unwrap the fish, which will fall apart, pick out the bones and put the fish back into the soup. And don't boil unscaled fish, even in a cloth.

Any food remains should be buried in a gash pit you've dug at least

Good effort by the recruits who built this: fallen tree used for the basha; good camouflage; basha kept low to preserve heat

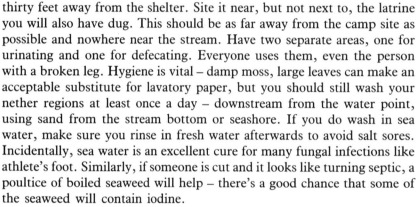

thirty feet away from the shelter. Site it near, but not next to, the latrine you will also have dug. This should be as far away from the camp site as possible and nowhere near the stream. Have two separate areas, one for urinating and one for defecating. Everyone uses them, even the person with a broken leg. Hygiene is vital – damp moss, large leaves can make an acceptable substitute for lavatory paper, but you should still wash your nether regions at least once a day – downstream from the water point, using sand from the stream bottom or seashore. If you do wash in sea water, make sure you rinse in fresh water afterwards to avoid salt sores. Incidentally, sea water is an excellent cure for many fungal infections like athlete's foot. Similarly, if someone is cut and it looks like turning septic, a poultice of boiled seaweed will help – there's a good chance that some of the seaweed will contain iodine.

And now for bed. Everybody bar none goes to the latrine before settling down for the night. The fire is then banked down – dry wood with dampish wood on top. A supply of kindling is handy to produce a blaze from the coals in the morning. If you have any doubts at all about your collective ability to keep the fire going, someone must always stay awake to make sure it doesn't go out. Work on the premise that you only have the one match or the one go with the lighter. Next, the two of you who have been doing all the work get into your dry clothes. Take the plastic sheeting and put it over the branches and leaves covering the floor. Use just enough to cover the floor only. Position the two injured in the middle, and the two fit ones on the outsides. Then wrap the remainder of the plastic sheet around all of you, but not so tightly as to prevent sweat vapour from escaping. The combined heat from your bodies should keep you all warm.

So far so good – you've all survived maybe your first two days in the wild. But the injured are causing concern – one of you has to go for help. Spend the day before you go reconnoitring the track you're going to use. Start at first light, go as far as you can until midday and then come back. This is because when you do go, you're going to leave at night – hopefully a clear, bright night – in order to let you cross the mountains by daylight.

Ten out of ten for scavenging –
but the basha is too high; plastic
sheeting needs covering to
avoid being blown away

So you need to know as much of the track as possible since you'll be using it in the dark – remember the old military maxim: time spent in reconnaissance is seldom wasted. The day before you set off, dead grass has been gathered and dried before the fire. This you'll stuff inside your clothing, next to your skin. If it's possible, swap your shoes for a pair a size larger, and stuff those with dried grass as well. It'll probably itch, but it should keep you warm. Take the oilskins, but don't wear them unless you absolutely must – again, your sweat vapour will condense inside and you'll get damp. If someone has a pair of thick woollen socks, you take them. Either you can use them as gloves, or – more importantly – if it suddenly freezes and you find yourself struggling over ice, you can put them over your shoes and they'll help to stop you slipping. Get a good stout stick and set off.

The plan is for you to follow the track. And you'll do just that. Even if it looks like going in the wrong direction, you stay with it. The only possible reason you can have for leaving it is if you see a house or an obvious road in the distance. If you do leave the track, you will leave some indication of the direction you've gone in – preferably a cairn of stones. Certainly it will be a sign that everyone back at the camp knows about. Similarly, as you go along the track, try to blaze some sort of trail every half mile or so – a few stones in arrow formation, say, pointing in the direction you've come from. The reasons for all this are fairly straightforward.

First, it may well be that your companions are rescued within a few hours of you setting off – and the rescuers will want to set off up the track after you. So if you have left it, they'll want to know in what direction – in case you've fallen into a gulley, or got trapped in a marsh. Similarly, if you're discovered by rescuers coming from the other direction – or even a passing shepherd – it'll be important to know what direction you've come from. Particularly if you're dead or unconscious when found – from exposure or from a fall. If you have any writing materials on you, make a note of where your companions are and put it into a dry pocket.

One final point. If you do go off the track and on to rough moorland, stay away from the edges of pools or surface streams – that's where the marshes are. Overall, don't travel unless you can see at least ten feet in front of you on the track and at least a quarter of a mile in front of you in open country – enough so you can recognize landmarks. And the next time you're sailing in rough weather, make sure you have a waterproof survival pack always handy. Similarly, never go hiking unless you're prepared to spend the night in the open – take a survival bag, chocolate, nuts and raisins, a lightweight portable stove, metal cup, tea bags and sugar, torch, waterproof matches, compass and map. At the most you're looking at possibly three extra pounds to carry. It could save your life.

Minimizing the risks

There is a deal of difference between military and civilian survival. But some of the lessons taught by the Royal Marines do have particular relevance to civilians, particularly those involved in outdoor activities like walking, climbing or skiing. And while it's true that many walkers, climbers or skiers can take care of themselves, a surprisingly large number can't – especially the 'amateurs', those who are possibly trying it for the first time. Or even experienced people who think that they don't have to worry too much because nothing bad will ever happen to them. Well it can, and it does. Every year, people suffer injury because what was intended as a gentle stroll in the foothills or across the moors turned into a nightmare when a sudden mist came down. Or a rain squall blew up out of nowhere. Or someone slipped, twisted an ankle – and a two-hour stroll turned into an eight-hour slog.

In Britain, many people die every year from exposure and some may even suffer frostbite, quite needlessly. Another big killer is avalanches. Reading this chapter will not necessarily save your life in these situations, but if it succeeds in making you more aware of the dangers, and how to overcome them, it'll prove well worthwhile. Aside from anything else, understanding the dangers gives you much more freedom to enjoy the wilderness. Before looking at exposure, frostbite and avalanches in some detail, a word of warning: don't try to do anything that's beyond your capabilities. Not many people can walk a straight ten or fifteen miles across open moorland without experiencing some difficulty, so don't take on too much. And always be prepared for the worst. It might be a beautiful day, but carry a pack containing at least waterproofs and a survival bag – plus spare compass and a map – if you're planning a long trek.

This chapter is based on the teaching of the Mountain and Arctic Warfare Cadre. However, not all their rules have been given, for the simple reason that too much knowledge could encourage a false sense of security. For example, the Cadre teaches a 'safe' way of crossing an avalanche slope – simply because that type of action is sometimes necessary in time of war. But there is no safe way of crossing an avalanche slope. The Cadre's method isn't so much safe as a way of trying to minimize the risks. Again, much of the Cadre's teaching presupposes a high degree of physical fitness, together with a basic knowledge of first aid and already well-honed survival skills. It's unreasonable, and probably downright dangerous, to expect the average reader to possess those attributes. The last thing one wants to do is give anyone a false sense of security – the feeling that 'now I've read the book, I can go and climb the nearest mountain'. Or disappear into the wilds for weeks on end. Or ski away from the accepted trails and runs. There is a world of difference between knowing something in theory and being able to do it in practice – in a way it's similar to the problem of being able to recognize an edible plant from a book illustration.

So don't, please, rush out and make like Royal Marines in the wilderness on the basis of reading this chapter. If you're that keen, join a recognized club. Or there's always your local Royal Marine Reserve. . . .

Exposure
Exposure is when the 'core' of your body cools down below the level at which your brain and muscular system can operate. It's caused by a combination of: cold; wind; moisture in the air (rain, snow, sleet, fog, spray, etc.); wet clothing; tiredness; anxiety; illness or injury; over-exertion (carrying too heavy a load, trying to walk/climb too far, etc.); not enough food or water; bad planning and simply trying to do far too much.

The symptoms are easily recognizable. First of all the victim feels chilly and his skin feels numb. He will start to shiver and find that his muscular co-ordination has begun to suffer, particularly in the hands. Next, he'll begin to feel weak, the lack of muscular co-ordination will intensify, he'll begin to stumble and show signs of mild confusion.

The next stage sees him stumble even more, to the point of falling over. Both his thoughts and speech will appear slow and halting. Then he stops shivering. However, he's unable to walk or stand and appears both incoherent and irrational. From there he lapses into semi-consciousness, with dilated pupils and a weak heart-beat or pulse. Finally he lapses into complete unconsciousness and will probably die due to heart failure.

The only way to prevent exposure is to fully understand and be able to recognize all its symptoms – and to realize that you don't have to be caught out in an arctic blizzard to die from it. You should also make sure that when you're out in the wilds you always carry the right equipment; that you eat and drink enough, remembering that salt reduces dehydration, so use it; that you're properly dressed and that you understand the wind-chill factor: that the wind can produce the effect of freezing temperatures even though the actual temperature is well above freezing.

Treatment is reasonably straightforward, but you must be able to recognize the early symptoms, as the body temperature continues to fall for one to two hours after treatment has begun. If someone is showing the first-stage symptoms, get them to the nearest shelter as soon as possible, get them into warm, dry clothing – build a fire if at all possible – and give them warm but not hot drinks, since too hot a drink will cause tissue damage. This is assuming that the nearest shelter is reachable before the second-stage symptoms occur. If it's not, you go right into the second-stage treatment.

You stop and provide some sort of shelter – even if it's just a large survival bag. Get the casualty into dry clothes and zip two sleeping bags together if you have them. Then get the casualty into the bags with a companion who's also dressed in dry clothes. Give the casualty any sugary food you have and a warm drink. When they recover, continue to treat them as injured and get them back to civilization – preferably on a stretcher if it can be arranged – as soon as possible. Never, ever give alcohol to someone suffering from exposure, since it will only worsen their condition. (If a friendly St Bernard appears with a keg of brandy use the brandy to light a fire and put the dog into the sleeping bag with the casualty.)

Do remember to cover the casualty's hands, feet, ears and nose, as anyone suffering from exposure is very susceptible to frostbite – and remember that ten per cent of your body heat is lost through your head: don't wait for really bad conditions before putting on a hat.

Frostbite

Frostbite occurs when parts of your body either freeze or partially freeze. It usually attacks the face, hands and feet. There are three degrees of frostbite. First, frostnip or localized frostbite, showing itself as dead white areas on the skin. Second, the skin ultimately blisters but doesn't die. Third, the flesh under the blisters dies.

Frostbite is obviously caused by cold temperatures. But the combination of cold plus wind plus moisture is the most dangerous – and the moisture can even be your own perspiration. The first symptom you'll be aware of is a feeling of cold and pain. Then comes the change of colour – white spots – in the skin, followed by total insensitivity in the afflicted part. Finally, you'll find it difficult to move your hand, foot or whatever.

The problem is that the insensitivity associated with second- and third-degree frostbite is very similar to the 'dead' feeling associated with frostnip. And the blisters from second-degree frostbite or the wounds from third-degree frostbite show only after the limb has thawed out. Many people have lost a finger, a toe and more simply because they thought it was only frostnip. So if you're in conditions that can cause frostbite, you must be particularly observant regarding yourself and your companions.

You can avoid frostbite reasonably easily. Make sure you always dress according to the weather conditions and what you expect to be doing. Try to avoid sweating (sweat=moisture=frostbite). If you have sweated, try to keep going until your clothes are dried out – and then put on extra clothing when you stop for a rest. Keep as active as you can, even down to exercising your face muscles, fingers and toes every now and then. This will help to keep them warm – and help you to detect any numb areas, i.e. the onset of frostbite. Make sure you get into shelter before you're exhausted. If you're camping out, brush all the loose snow from your clothes before you get into your tent – and make doubly sure that there's no loose snow inside your sleeping bag. The snow will melt, your clothing will get damp and you'll probably get frostbite the following day. Always make sure you've a spare pair of dry socks and mittens – and that they're both clean and dry. Eat as often as you can and take a warm drink as often as you can since this helps to keep your body temperature up.

Immediate treatment for frostnip or frostbite is fairly basic. Get out of the wind and put a warm hand on the part of your face – or that of a companion – that is frozen. If your hands are affected, put them under your armpits. If your feet are affected, you have to wait until you get back to proper shelter. Then take off your boots and socks and put your feet against the warm skin of a friend (which is when you discover who your friends really are). Whatever you do, don't rub the affected part – with snow or anything else. Don't use any ointment on it and don't expose it to any direct heat like a stove or a fire, since chilled flesh is very easily damaged.

The Royal Marines have a little mnemonic to teach the principles of keeping warm in extreme conditions:

Keep clothing	**C**lean
Avoid	**O**verheating
Dress loosely and in	**L**ayers
Keep clothing	**D**ry

Avalanches

Every year, hundreds of people die needlessly in avalanches – needlessly, because if they'd followed basic safety rules they'd never have been caught in an avalanche in the first place. Or if they had, they'd know how to have

Demonstrating a survival suit, a Marine in Norway swims from the (Dutch) LCVP, with the temperature around the minus thirty degrees Fahrenheit mark

the best chance of surviving. By virtue of their long experience in Northern Norway, the Royal Marines have become somewhat expert about avalanches – here, then, are their basic rules for survival:

- Keep as high up the slope as possible, since most avalanches are triggered by their very victims.
- Stay away from snow accumulation areas during and immediately after a snow storm.
- Remember that lee slopes are particularly prone to 'soft-slab' avalanches.
- Never travel alone and never expose more than one person in your party to an avalanche risk at any one time. And don't assume that just because someone else has successfully crossed a risk area that it's safe.
- Stay well away from snow cornices and the slopes beneath them.
- Remember that snow fractures take place on the convex part of the slope, and that the most dangerous slopes are those between thirty and forty-five degrees.
- If you do cross beneath a potential avalanche slope, keep well below the tree line – and listen to what the local experts have to tell you.
- Watch out for avalanche warning signs, like snow booming, heavy snow balling, fresh avalanche tracks, cracks appearing in the snow when you stand on it or even mini avalanches from your boots or skis. Remember that the deeper the snow, the greater the danger. Snow settling at more than one inch an hour means avalanche danger.
- Remember also that snow takes up to three days to settle properly, longer in cold weather and if it's out of the sun.

If you are caught in an avalanche there are a few things you can do other than offering up a quick prayer and wishing that you had been a better person. Get rid of your rucksack and skis (if you're wearing them) as soon as possible, although if you're a good skier you may be able to ski out of trouble. Then take the time to assess the avalanche and where you are in relation to it – at the top, bottom or middle, or to one side, and where your best escape route is. But don't try to escape immediately. Wait as long as you can, because the more snow that goes past you in the beginning, the less there'll be to bury you at the finish. If you are caught up in it, and swimming movements are possible, don't try the breaststroke or crawl. Apparently the most effective is the double back stroke with your back to the force of the avalanche. But overall, just try to ride it out as best you can, conserving your strength for the last few minutes. Keep your mouth closed and if you're in a powder-snow avalanche, cover your face with clothing to help you to breathe.

You'll feel the avalanche begin to lose momentum and settle. At this point don't try to fight towards the surface, just make an air space around your head so that you can breathe. When everything comes to a stop, don't immediately dig upwards. You may be digging downwards. There are two ways of finding out which direction is up. You can spit and see which way the saliva flows, or you can urinate and feel which way the urine goes. Whichever method, you dig in the opposite direction – and don't panic, because the greater the panic the greater the chance of developing exposure and indeed tiring yourself out. Dig slowly and sensibly, resting whenever you feel tired, to conserve your strength.

8/FIRST DRAFT

Leaving Lympstone is a joyous time for YO and recruit alike: the end to a very difficult year or six months, the right to be called Royal Marine Commandos – and the feeling that they've earned that right. But the joy is often tinged with a little apprehension, for as trained Marines their standards will be expected to be that much higher. No excuses, or rather allowances, are made for the fact that the man's still only a beginner (not that many allowances ever were made). Life in a troop will be altogether harsher and more unforgiving for the newcomer until he begins to show signs of coming to grips with his job.

Generally speaking, the first stop after Lympstone is a troop – unless a recruit has been 'persuaded' to apply for driver or clerk training. (There is a serious shortage of clerks in the Corps, which is hardly surprising since few men join the Marines to fight a desk. It does appear that perhaps this is one function that could best be done by Royal Navy personnel.)

The young officer who goes to a troop for the first time will be left under no illusion by his OC or commanding officer that his studies are still continuing. The Corp's attitude on this is best illustrated by the Company Commander (a major) who called a new troop sergeant into his office to explain his duties as he, the OC, saw them.

The sergeant was there to run the troop and train the new troop officer. If the sergeant had any problems with the new officer, he was to let the OC know via the sergeant major, and the OC would sort them out instantly. But this approach does not mean that a sergeant can take liberties with a new officer; the troop sergeant's job is to train that young man up to the point where he could run the troop himself. Unfortunately, young officers never have long enough with a troop to fully learn this specific aspect of soldiering as well as they – and their men – would like.

The relationship that develops, or should develop, between officer and sergeant is one of the most important in the officer's life. It must be based on mutual trust and respect. And since the sergeant will often be several years older than the officer, a certain fatherly – or rather, big brotherly – attitude is bound to creep in.

In describing this, one senior officer remembered the time that his troop first invited him out for a drink with the lads. This is a time-honoured Corps custom which lets an officer know that he's been accepted – and on this one occasion ended with the sergeant throwing the officer over his shoulder and carrying him back to the officers' mess. A slightly extreme example, perhaps, but it does emphasize that a troop sergeant does have a responsibility for a new officer – a responsibility to keep him out of trouble as much as teach him his trade.

The other major problem for YO and young Marine alike is discovering how little they do actually know, no matter that they've passed out of Lympstone. Time was that Marines first sent to a unit were put in the charge of an experienced Marine, whom they had to refer to as 'Trained

Soldier' for at least the first year. Things are a little bit more relaxed these days, but a sprog Marine is still a sprog Marine – and if he's spared the annoyance of being told what to do by someone without any rank, he has to work that much harder on his own, has to accept that much more responsibility since he's very much thrown in at the deep end.

Suddenly, he discovers that the thirty-miler is nothing in comparison to what he'll be expected to do in Norway. The three-week Arctic Warfare course is not too bad, and the accent is very much on the practical, so it can be an absorbing, though tiring, time. But when he gets to a unit and discovers that he's expected to be able to ski (cross country) fifty kilometres, carrying anything up to a hundred and twenty pounds, that's when it really begins to hurt. It probably takes at least two years to build up the stamina needed to operate effectively as a Royal Marine in Northern Norway, and at least that long to learn how to ski cross country properly. After all, with over a hundred pounds on one's back, it's that much easier to fall over – and that much harder to get up and get started again.

Company patrol in Norway.
Note how well spread out along
the track they are; also the size
of their bergens – each man
carries well over 100 pounds on
his back

But there again, there is considerable criticism within the Corps that Marines do carry so much weight on their backs, since it often leads to knee and back problems at quite an early age. Part of the problem is that young Marines tend to go out with more kit than they really need. But the major problem is that military equipment is traditionally heavy and bulky and is often developed by people without any real practical experience. It also takes far too long for the latest technology to filter through, and the military research and development departments often appear to be stubborn in their refusal to buy direct from an outside source without spending time and money on their own development procedures. The simple truth is that many companies do manufacture kit for the civilian market (admittedly the civilian specialized market of mountaineering or trekking) that is usable by the military, albeit with a few minor changes. This is one reason why the supremely professional units, like the Royal Marines or Paras, turn a blind eye to unofficial equipment as long as it's being used for practical reasons and not because it's become fashionable – an attitude that is intensely disliked in many military research and development circles, since every non-issue pair of boots worn, for example, points out their own failure to provide the right equipment.

However, the Royal Marines take comfort from the fact that the USMC is in a far worse position, particularly vis-à-vis Norway. Not only do they suffer from the 'it must be American' proviso that affects the use of all kit by US forces, the USMC also forbids *any* non-issue kit. So whereas a Royal Marine in the field in Northern Norway will be wearing Norwegian Army roll-top shirts and thick sweaters, possibly British civilian climbing boots, even Finnish cross-country ski boots – all kit designed to keep a man safe in those conditions – the US Marine will be suffering from the issue of cold-weather gear that might be effective in the High Sierras, New England or even the Yukon, but has little or no relevance to weather conditions in Norway – where it can be minus forty Fahrenheit one day with driving blizzards, and plus two the next with driving rain, followed by a sudden freeze back down to minus forty.

One of the more stimulating aspects of arctic training for the novice YO or Marine is the ice swim. Its origins lie in the supposition that at any time, any man may break through the ice into the water below – and that he'd better know how to get himself out of it. The technique is fairly simple.

For demonstration purposes, a Mountain Leader has already cut a hole in the ice with a chain saw (they used to use explosives but it all got out of hand . . .). Then, the same Mountain Leader demonstrates the technique.

He skis towards the hole in the ice, fully equipped, and into the water. (Not leaping in while holding his nose and crying 'For the honour of the Regiment!' as one British soldier did recently.) He then kicks off his skis, shrugs his way out of his bergen – which he tries to put on to the safe ice around him – and then uses his ski-poles (which must never be let go) to lever his way out of the water and on to the ice.

Depending on the weather conditions, his mates then have up to two minutes to get him out of his wet clothes (which will probably freeze solid as soon as he's in the open air) and into a dry set.

But breaking through the ice on a river or lake is not the worst danger.

At least you have a reasonably good chance of getting out, assuming that the current isn't so strong that it will sweep you away; that you're fit enough and well trained enough to withstand the sudden shock of falling into extremely cold water; that your companions have the presence of mind to be getting dry clothing out of their bergens while you're still struggling to get out of the water; or that if you're alone, and have managed to get your own bergen to safety, that you've had the forethought to have a dry change of clothes safely wrapped in a waterproof bag. Assuming all that, falling in shouldn't pose too much of a problem.

As a Mountain Leader explained: 'There's no real way of knowing if river or lake ice is safe or not – although after a time, you do develop a sixth sense about it. But breaking through into the water isn't the worst thing. Up in the mountains there are a lot of reservoirs or small lakes that go on draining away long after an ice crust has formed. So you get an ice roof and nothing beneath it. Break through that, and it's a long drop to the rocky floor below.

'And you also get the situation where the weight of the snow has pressed the ice surface down below the waterline, and the water has seeped on to the surface from the edges of a lake. So there's maybe six or seven feet of snow and beneath that several feet of slush before you reach the ice. It's possible to drown in that slush, or at the best get wet feet, which can be pretty dangerous.

'Basically, if you're not on skis you should be on snowshoes outside the camp, unless you know the area very, very well. Even then, you can be walking on what you think is hard-packed snow and suddenly you'll hit a soft spot – easy to sprain a knee or an ankle that way.'

Snowholes are dug into a deep bank of snow and there is a strict procedure for digging them. First of all the troop leader finds an area with enough snow by using his avalanche probe. Then the men who're going to do the actual digging take off as many clothes as they can – on a bright day, they'll strip down to trousers and boots. This is because they'll sweat while digging and it's very hard to dry clothes in minus temperatures. Two shovels are always used, although only one is ever inside the snowhole at any one time – you'll see why in a moment. Two men carve out a doorway, usually about six feet high by three feet wide. The size doesn't matter because it can be filled in later. One man then digs straight into the side of the bank for some ten to fifteen feet, depending on how many men are going to be living there. When he's got as far as he needs to, he turns to his right and begins to dig out a shelf, starting at about waist level. This will be expanded, and will form the living quarters. The roof will be arched and ribbed, so that any melt water will run down the ribs, rather than drip on to the men. He'll probably also carve a niche for a candle and finally poke a ski pole through the roof into the open air to provide ventilation.

Obviously, the same man or men don't do all the digging. But someone always stays outside with a spare shovel in case the hole collapses and buries the digger in snow. Similarly, a shovel is always left outside in case the hole collapses when it's being used, and the sentries can then dig out the occupants. Finally, the main doorway will be partially blocked off from the top, making a tunnel through which you have to crawl to get inside.

Learning how to cope with an ice break . . . ski-poles held shoulder high and to his front, a Marine struggles towards safe ice

A patrol moves warily along a
corniced snow ridge, making for
their RV with a Rigid Raider
(below).
Opposite: Marine's eye view
through the standard gas mask

The living accommodation – the shelf – is higher than the actual floor of the snowhole and since warm air rises, the coldest air remains below the shelf. The candle must be lit whenever the snowhole's being used. At night, there will always be a minimum of two sentries who will check the snowholes together, making sure that there hasn't been a cave-in or that the occupants aren't suffocating because of cooker fumes or a blocked ventilation shaft. When the sentries do check the snowholes, one of them always waits outside – again, in case of a cave-in. Survival in the Arctic is an infinite capacity for taking pains.

Cooking is done with naphtha-fuelled stoves, since paraffin will turn to jelly at very low temperatures. Arctic ration packs feature freeze-dried food, lots of coffee and tea, the ubiquitous packet of Rolos – someone in the MoD must have shares in the company that makes them – the ever-present five pieces of hard lavatory paper, plus the usual assortment of glucose tablets, matches, etc. There can be an awful sameness about Arctic ration packs, but for all that, the food ain't bad – in fact, the rolled oatmeal flakes mixed with dried apple flakes can be warmly recommended for breakfast, particularly since they can be cooked in the bag, as it were – boiling water poured directly into the packet, rather than mixing every-thing together in a mess tin, which only means more washing up.

There is a set procedure for cooking in the field, designed to save time and fuel. The main meal is always at night. Using the buddy system, one man cooks for two, both usually sharing the same mess tin, which saves washing up (i.e. saves fuel and time). While the meal is being eaten, water will also be boiled – and that will be used to make a hot drink which will be put in a Thermos flask for breakfast. So come breakfast, all the men have to do is prepare their oatmeal and apple flakes, and make another hot drink in the Thermos to be carried with them for use during the day. Hot water is never used for shaving – 'wet' razors should never be used in the Arctic since nicks and scrapes do not heal properly in low temperatures. Battery razors are the rule, and every man must shave – not because beards are illegal, but because a beard disguises the telltale signs of frostbite.

Above and below left: Emphasizing the problems of beach landings in the Arctic, an FH70 bogs down in Northern Norway.

Even the mat laying Eager Beaver had its problems – both vehicles finally rescued by the tracked Beach Recovery Vehicle (below)

The camp itself will either be a snowhole, a bivvy made from tentsheets (lozenge-shaped pieces of canvas, carried one per man, which clip together in a variety of configurations depending on the size of 'tent' required), or possibly a brushwood bivvy, constructed so that the heat from the fire burning outside is reflected back into the bivvy by an improvised windbreak.

Norway is a tough few months – as an officer explained: 'People at home [civilians] don't realize quite how hard the boys work out here, or what the conditions are like. Look at 42 Commando – very few of those guys will see a woman for the whole three or so months they're out here. It's one continual slog, with only Saturday night – and not always then – to relax in the NAAFI bar. Sunday, they're getting ready to go back out in the field again. 45 Commando have it a little bit easier because they're nearer a major town [Narvik] but even then the opportunities for rest and relaxation are extremely limited. It's the equivalent of mounting a major polar expedition year after year. The pressures on the Corps are so great that we don't have the time to make it easier for the lads.'

This brings us to the subject of Royal Marines misbehaving when they get amongst the innocent Norwegian civilians. Every year there's at least one horror story, usually wildly inaccurate, which has the unfortunate result of breeding a very defensive attitude on the part of the Corps. For example, in 1986 it was widely reported that Royal Marines from 45 Commando had indulged in 'homosexual' orgies in a bar in Narvik. The story was first run by a local newspaper and picked up (some six weeks later) by the British tabloid press.

What actually happened is that a group of Royal Marines, admittedly in a, well, happy frame of mind, treated other drinkers to a rendition of 'Old MacDonald had a Farm' and 'Zulu Warrior', two Corps favourites which, as any rugby player will tell you, for some reason result in someone stripping off all his clothes. Slightly crude maybe, but a homosexual orgy it's not.

What isn't generally appreciated by the press outside Norway is that of the more than one hundred and thirty newspapers there, well over half are extremely left wing. And of those, many are anti-NATO – certainly anti-military. There are several newspapers around Narvik like this (nearly every inhabited valley in Northern Norway has its own newspaper, and 5000 would be considered a good circulation) who frankly seize on every opportunity to discredit the Corps. The average Marine is not some sort of an angel, and in a Corps numbering over seven thousand, you will find the occasional unpleasant character. But by and large, the stories of bestial behaviour are exaggerated. Nor are the Norwegian population totally without blame, particularly the men.

For all its image as a socialist paradise, Norway does have one or two glaring faults. Aside from being one of the most expensive countries in Europe, it also has the highest rate of wife-beating. Norwegian men often tend to be dour, taking themselves extremely seriously and looking upon foreign males as markedly less civilized. Unfortunately, Norwegian women – or at least a high percentage of them – appear to enjoy the company of the Royal Marines. They make them laugh and often treat them with a courtesy sadly lacking in their own menfolk.

'I don't know, even after all these years, if it's just their way or if they're trying to be deliberately rude,' explained a Royal Marine officer, 'but a Norwegian male will often simply push through a group of Royals and local girls without saying excuse me, or smiling – just barge through. Either way, I must admit I find it slightly reprehensible and I'm afraid the lads do as well. I think you'll find that in most fights involving Norwegian civilians, the local men are just as much to blame as our lads. Which doesn't excuse Royal, but it would be nice if occasionally the press back home realized that there are two sides to every story. Aside from anything else, if a Royal Marine is found to have caused trouble, without any provocation, he's likely to be sent home. That means he'll miss the extra pay and allowances he gets for coming to Norway in the first place – and that can hurt.'

Certainly the local Norwegian authorities do go to some lengths to protect their womenfolk from the invading barbarian hordes. On one – perhaps apocryphal – occasion, the mayor of a town complained to the

Below: Demonstrating how much the new BV's can carry – an anti-tank section plus all their kit

Right: Standard Arctic 'rat-pack'. Note high sugar/glucose content, including the inevitable tube of Rolos (NB: toffee is not the most sensible sweet to issue in below zero temperatures). While the main meal does vary, one unlucky Marine in the Falklands drew nothing but Chicken Supreme for six weeks!

Overleaf: Moving out to establish a beach head perimeter, a 'Cloggy' encounters deep snow

Marines that girls younger than the legal age of eighteen were drinking in the Royal Marine bar.

'Well,' said an ever-helpful Marine, 'maybe you should give us a list of all the girls who are old enough to drink in our bars, that way we'll be able to double check their ID.'

The mayor thought this a great idea and produced a list of names and addresses. Within twenty-four hours every woman on it had been issued a personal invitation to a Marines party the following weekend.

'I don't know why the mayor got so upset about it,' said one of the Marines, 'we were only trying to be helpful. . . .'

The basic kit

For those of you who are interested, here's the basic kit that a Royal Marine will carry in his bergen (actually a Crusader-pattern rucksack) in the Arctic:

> Minimum one day's rations
> Duvet boots
> Quilted suit (known as a Mao suit)
> Waterproof outers
> Sleeping bag
> Waterproof bivvie bag
> Sleeping mat
> Mess tin
> Metal mug ('gaffer' or masking tape applied to the mug edge to avoid burning the lips)
> Spoon (preferably strong plastic to avoid heat or cold burns)
> Fuel can (naphtha)
> Cooker
> Funnel
> Snowbrush (hard-bristled, used to brush snow off equipment, clothes, sleeping mat, etc.)
> Unbreakable Thermos flask
> Battery shaver
> Toothbrush and paste
> Candles (used to provide basic heat and light inside a snowhole or other bivvie)
> Meta-tabs (to light stove)
> Moon boots
> Six pairs of spare socks
> Spare shirt
> Camouflage outers
> Tent or tent sheets
> Toe caps

Some words of explanation:

Duvet boots are ankle-height padded bootees, used when the Marine is inside his snowhole or bivvie – he'll probably also wear them for sleeping – as he will the quilted Mao suit, although this can also be worn under his outer clothes if he's on sentry duty. Moon boots are very large boot covers, made from canvas and an insulating material. They can be worn over regular boots or duvet boots. For example, if a man needs to use the latrine in the middle of the night, rather than go to all the trouble of putting his regular boots back on, he can simply slip on the moon boots over his duvet boots. Toe caps are canvas and rubber 'slip overs', and are worn when the man is fairly stationary outside, since the foot loses heat from the toe area more quickly than from the heel.

There is, naturally, an optimum way of packing a bergen:

To begin with, all spare clothing is rolled up tight and secured with masking tape – this makes it considerably easier to pack. The sleeping bag plus waterproof outer is carried at the base of the pack – duvet boots rolled up inside.

Starting from the bottom of the bergen, the man will pack his spare clothing, then his windproof bottoms (he wears the windproof jacket), then a spare shirt, spare socks, moon boots, Mao suit, and his flask on top – in other words, all items accessible in the order they're most likely to be needed. In the large pocket on the back of the bergen will be packed a snowbrush, battery shaver, toothbrush and paste and tomorrow's breakfast meal – items that won't be needed until last thing at night. In the left-hand side pocket will be the fuel can, cooker, funnel, Meta-tabs and candles – all inflammable items together. His sleeping mat goes under the hood of the bergen, and if he's carrying a tent or tentsheet(s), they'll be secured on top. Finally, inside the top pocket will be his spare hat and gloves, in plastic. All the clothing items will also be carefully waterproofed.

Now, as to how he's dressed:

First, he'll be wearing thermal underwear. Then, at least two pairs of thermal socks. Then, standard trousers, probably a Norwegian-issue shirt, a pullover, windproof jacket with hood (hood rolled down inside the collar when not in use), boots with a special welt for cross-country skiing, Gortex gaiters from boot to knee, inner gloves, outer wool gloves and windproof glove covers. He'll also be carrying special gloves used when filling the stove or touching bare metal. He may also be using camouflage mittens.

Obviously, not all this clothing will be worn at the same time – he'll discard this or that layer, depending on how hard he's working. When gloves are not being worn, they're always tucked inside the top of his jacket – they're never put on to the ground, nor is the hat.

Finally, one other piece of kit which for all its simplicity is probably one of the finest inventions ever – the headover. Essentially a wide woollen sleeve the headover is worn around the neck as a scarf. It can also be worn over the neck and head, or twisted and worn around the ears. It's extremely versatile and whoever thought of it deserves a medal.

The Marine will also be carrying a shovel, his personal weapon, spare ammunition, probably spare ammunition for the section weapon or spare batteries for the radio, snowshoes and any other little creature comforts that he feels like carrying. Altogether, he'll be carrying on his back and on his person well over a hundred pounds in weight. And incidentally, the total cost of his arctic kit is well over £1,000 – which makes losing it an expensive business.

The total weight of all his equipment – official issue plus personal items – is likely to exceed one hundred and twenty pounds – probably nearer a hundred and thirty. That's approximately nine stone to be carried, on skis, up and down hill, day in day out for three months in weather conditions ranging from freezing rain to blizzards, from plus seven degrees to minus twenty or thirty Fahrenheit. It's hardly surprising that the average age of a Royal Marine rifleman is twenty.

9/ROYAL AT WAR

The exhaustion shows as
J Company moves into Port
Stanley

Sooner or later the training is invariably put to the test. Sometimes it's in a one-off situation like the Falklands War, an operation that stretched 3 Commando Brigade to the utmost. At other times it's a war that drags on and on. A war that the nation would rather forget, and for which there are no bunting-strewn celebrations when the boys come home. A war like Northern Ireland's

The Royal Marines have never been found wanting in bravery. They do not, however, believe in the pointless death – the *folie de grandeur* of the Death or Glory Charge against insurmountable odds that tends to obscure the fact that something has gone seriously wrong.

The Royal Marines do not believe that dying well is the point of war. They believe in winning; in achieving their objectives as safely as possible, by using every means at their disposal. Not least of those means are the courage and aggression of the men who fight – but never in isolation, never divorced from intellect and imagination.

A senior Royal Navy officer who served 'down South' found himself extremely impressed by 'Royal's caution': when the Marines were faced with an enemy strongpoint, they'd assess the problem before rushing off to attack it. They always considered how to take an objective with the minimum of their own casualties. Interestingly enough, this rarely if ever slowed up the Marines, since there was less chance of them becoming bogged down by enemy fire. A Royal Marine officer remembered watching his men fighting along the top of Mount Harriet, and being amused by the way, whenever they reached an Argentinian fortified position, they'd duck round behind the nearest rock, maybe have a quick puff at a cigarette, think about the problem for a few minutes – and then suddenly swing into action with tremendous speed, efficiency and even ferocity.

This almost surgical approach, this recognition that war is really about destroying the enemy and that the Marines were there to take back the Falklands by destroying the Argentinians, did not always sit well with those at home who were unwilling to accept the reality that fighting a war means killing.

Nor, for that matter, does the style of the Royal Marines always sit well with soldiers from elsewhere in the British armed forces (who often complain of Royal's arrogance) since the Marine approach requires great independence and initiative – sometimes bloodyminded independence and initiative – on the part of the most junior Marine. This does not always please those accustomed to a more docile type of soldier – nor indeed those accustomed to a more docile type of officer. Not that this applied to relations between the Marines and the Paras – one of the more gratifying results from the Falklands was the recognition of the respect that existed between the Royal Marines and the Parachute Regiment.

As a Marine senior NCO said recently: 'The Paras are pretty much like us, really. Very professional and simply wanting to get the job done as quickly as possible. There'll always be rivalry of some sort – it's only natural, particularly amongst the young soldiers and Marines. But the relationship between the older guys is excellent. I know that there's no one else I'd rather go into battle alongside. If there is a difference, it's that we probably think a little bit more about a problem at troop and even section level. But that reflects the training and the different roles – Paras have to go for broke because you can't really disguise a Para drop, whereas we're trained as much to infiltrate – to be that little more sneaky. But I don't like to hear anyone slagging the Paras off, even a Marine. They're good soldiers and our guys'll fight alongside them any time.'

When looking at the Falklands it's a little difficult to isolate those characteristics that make the Royal Marines special – simply because they tend to be the ones that all soldiers are supposed to possess. Nor does one want to get into a Royal Marine versus Para argument – that kind of comparison is invidious and self-defeating. It is tempting to compare and contrast the Marines with, say, the Scots or Welsh Guards – but neither of those two regiments were trained for the Falklands conflict to quite the same extent as were the Marines, and neither was as heavily involved; and one would expect the Marines to be better anyway, particularly in an amphibious operation. None the less, the Falklands War was very much 3 Commando Brigade's war, if only because 3 Commando Brigade staff were responsible for most of the planning and execution. Again, this is not taking anything away from the Paras, the SAS, or any other attached army units.

Royal Marines like to characterize themselves as 'the thinking man's infantry'. Add to this their ability to improvize – their flexibility – and their discipline plus their endurance, and you have many of the reasons why the Falklands were recaptured when all academic military logic suggested that the Argentinians could have performed far better – or even possibly won.

Of course, the effectiveness of the Royal Marines as a fighting force had been demonstrated when Argentina invaded South Georgia and the Falkland Islands. On South Georgia, the Royal Marines shot down one troop-carrying helicopter and one Alouette helicopter, and crippled one corvette. On the Falklands, Royal Marines had taken out one Amtrak (armoured, tracked personnel carrier), captured three prisoners (Argentinian Special Forces who'd broken into Government House) and wounded seventeen and marked three known kills – excluding those men in the Amtrak. All this without losing a single man.

During the planning for the Falklands War, 3 Commando Brigade were promised that the air battle would be won before the landings were to take place. This didn't mean that the entire Argentinian Air Force would be wiped out, merely that casualties due to air attacks could be kept to

42 Commando on the long yomp towards Mount Kent

manageable proportions. As a result, it had been planned that the task force ships would be kept in close logistical support and that *Canberra*, in particular, would be used as a field dressing station. Unless they remain secret, amphibious landings require air parity if not superiority. In the event, this was not the case.

For a variety of reasons, notably the fear of submarine attacks which kept ships at sea, it hadn't been possible to test-fire Rapier (anti-aircraft missile system) during April 1982 at Ascension Island where the task force had gathered to restow, to train and to wait for intelligence being gathered on South Georgia and the Falklands by the SBS and SAS (who, officially, began operating in the Falklands on 2 May). Not only that, but Rapier had been crammed into the ships' holds, with people scrambling all over it, and experiencing temperatures that ranged from 120 degrees to 0 degrees Fahrenheit on the trip from Ascension to the Falklands. This is not the best way of treating sensitive electronic equipment.

As a result, when Rapier was finally deployed following the landings on 21 May, out of the ten Rapiers on shore, only six were actually ready to fire, in spite of the almost heroic efforts of their crews to get them into position and into commission. It was estimated afterwards that it would have needed at least twenty Rapiers to do a proper job – still not totally denying air space to the Argentinians, but certainly not incurring the losses that the task force did. And then there was the bravery and skill of the Argentinian pilots themselves.

As one of the Rapier officers said: 'We'd trained for a war in Germany, with aircraft coming in at 250 feet doing a maximum 350 knots. And there were those guys coming in at 100 feet doing 450 knots. It took us a little time to work out how to handle them.'

Eventually the Rapier crews and the Harrier pilots did work out how to handle the Argentinian aircraft. But not until the *Atlantic Conveyor* (amongst others) had been sunk. And not until task force ships like the *Canberra* had been sent away to the edge of the Total Exclusion Zone, well out of Exocet range. Sunk with the *Atlantic Conveyor* were three Chinook and five Wessex helicopters – vital for moving stores and equipment. Sailed away with the *Canberra* were all the unit stores of 40 Commando, 42 Commando and 3 Para, plus the equivalent of 90,000 man days of rations. The *Canberra* was not to make its reappearance until hostilities were over – which obviously denied its use as a field dressing station.

It's bad enough to lose so many stores, so much vital equipment at the best of times – when you're in a position to be easily resupplied. In the South Atlantic, thousands of miles away from any resupply base, it could have been, probably should have been, fatal. That it wasn't was as much due to a little-known Royal Marine unit as it was to the fighting qualities of the Royal Marines or the Paras themselves. And this unit's very existence emphasizes how different the Marines are.

Commando Logistical Regiment Royal Marines was formed between July 1971 and January 1972. During this time, existing logistic elements from 3 Commando Brigade and administrative elements from HQ Commando forces were gathered together and given their own separate identity. Commando Logs (as it's known) exists to provide second-line medical, transport, ordnance and workshop support. It's primarily com-

A hot, rolled-oat and apple flake breakfast at ten degrees Fahrenheit on Mount Kent. Note how the hot water is poured into the bag, rather than mixing the meal up in a mess tin – quicker and cleaner

LOGISTICIANS (according to Cdo Log Regt)

The role of the logistician in war is appreciated by very few. The Commando Logistic Regiment Royal Marines explain it in this way (without claiming original authorship):

'Logisticians are a sad, embittered race of men, very much in demand in war [but] who sink resentfully into obscurity in peace.

'They deal only with facts but must work for men who merchant in theories. They emerge in war because war is very much fact. They disappear in peace because in peace, war is mostly theory. Generals are the people who merchant in theories, who employ logisticians in war and ignore them in peace. Logisticians hate generals. Generals are a happily blessed race who radiate confidence and power, feeding only on ambrosia and drinking only nectar. They stride confidently forward in peace, invading countries simply by sweeping their hands over a map. In war they must stride more slowly because each general then has a logistician on his back who may, at any moment, lean forward and whisper: "No, you can't do that." Generals fear logisticians in war and try to forget about them in peace.

'Romping happily alongside generals are strategists and tacticians. Logisticians despise strategists and tacticians – who in turn do not know about logisticians, until they grow up and become generals. This they usually do.

'Sometimes a logistician gets to become a general. And then he must associate with other generals whom he hates, while listening to tacticians and strategists whom he despises, while on his own back he now has another logistician whom he fears. This is why logisticians who get stars on their shoulders also get ulcers and cannot eat their ambrosia.'

posed of Royal Marines; of those attached from either the army or navy, most if not all are commando trained. And although Commando Logs is unique in as much as it is commanded in turn by a Royal Marine or an army officer, it's still very much a Royal Marine concept. For in the army, all these various logistical units come under their own independent commands – engineers under the Royal Engineers, workshop units under the Engineers or Royal Electrical and Mechanical Engineers, stores and supply under the Royal Army Ordnance Corps or Royal Corps of Transport. In the Royal Marines, they all come under one roof, as it were.

Commando Logs exists to supply 3 Commando Brigade. But it can also produce – at literally a moment's notice – a smaller version of itself to support an individual commando that's operating independently or some distance away from its parent formation. And there can be no doubt that much of the success of the Falklands was due to the fact that Commando Logs coped brilliantly with disaster after disaster.

Soldiers – and Marines – in the front line are usually aware of the logistics units supplying them only when something doesn't turn up. Or the wrong thing turns up. Otherwise, they tend to treat resupply as a matter of course. In the Falklands, in the vast majority of cases supplies did turn up when and where they were needed. Considering that the Brigade was spread out over the island and that the lines of communication were harassed by Argentinian aircraft, and that Commando Logs had to supply all the units on the Islands, and that transport was at minimum as were supplies themselves, this was nothing short of miraculous. Except that a Marine would say that it was just another example of a unit doing the job they were trained for – no big deal, that's how they earn their pay.

Commando Logs works by first establishing a Beach Support Area (BSA), where stocks are held close to the beach landing area or port.

Then, as the Brigade moves forward, Commando Logs follows and sets up a secondary supply area – the Brigade Maintenance Area or BMA. If the forward unit gets very far forward, Commando Logs establishes a third supply area – the Forward Brigade Maintenance Area (FBMA). In the Falklands, the FBMA had been set up at Teal Inlet to support the final attack for Port Stanley – a distance of some thirty-four kilometres from San Carlos, over some of the worst terrain in the world. And all the while the BSA was under attack from Argentinian aircraft. Again, it was the flexibility of Commando Logs that allowed them to cope with the situation, that and the ability to stay cool at a moment of disaster, and immediately start figuring out a change in plan. In fact these are the same characteristics that you would find amongst all Marine units – but without Commando Logs those units wouldn't have been able to survive a day, let alone take Port Stanley.

From Commando Logs to the Commando himself – and a couple of examples of why a Royal Marine has the reputation that he does:

It's difficult and extremely dangerous to attack an enemy machine-gun position. Theoretically, it needs at least one troop (about thirty men) in three sections. One section provides covering fire while the other two attack. These are odds of thirty against three or four – and even then victory cannot be guaranteed. Certainly the troop will suffer casualties.

The Argentinians were well supplied with machine guns. And the Royal Marines decided not to use troop attacks on them, but to simply take them out using anti-tank rockets.

'It was,' as a Marine senior NCO said, 'something that the boys decided very quickly. It didn't come down from on high as a new piece of tactical thinking, it originated with the average Marine in a rifle section who didn't see why he should get shot up because that's what the book said. To me it's a good example of Royal using his imagination and initiative. And of course, being set up the way we are, it was dead easy for the guys to get the sixty-sixes or eighty-fours they needed [66 mm Light Anti-Tank Weapon and 84 mm Medium Anti-Tank Weapon, used at section level]. Like, I would imagine that in an army regiment, it wouldn't be so easy. But with us, all the guys had to do was go and ask for the kit, and there it was. And then we had crateloads of rockets being sent down from the UK. With never a tank in sight.'

From that it was but a short step to using anti-tank weapons to clear enemy trenches, a practice that became increasingly common. Aside from the fact that it worked, it also demonstrated that the Marines – and also the Paras – had lost patience with the Argentinian method of fighting. Argentinian troops tended to fire at anything that moved (on at least one occasion when a neighbouring trench was showing a white flag, and on another when an officer had moved forward, also under a white flag, to offer them terms of surrender) until British troops came dangerously close to them, at which point they would either 'cower in the bottom of their trench or immediately surrender'. So it was that the Marines saw them as being badly trained and easily demoralized, and fought them with a certain degree of contempt.

42 Commando used anti-tank rockets against Argentinian machine guns in its attack on Mount Harriet – except in this instance, MILAN anti-tank

A CASEVAC at a Medical Aid Station, the casualty brought in by a Scout helicopter

missiles were chosen. J Company, 42 Commando, set up a diversionary attack, hoping that the Argentinians would reply with all their machine guns, thus pinpointing the enemy positions. And, since MILAN did not have night sights at that time, 42 Commando would use mortar illumination to aid the MILAN crews' aim at their targets. It was a superb piece of tactical improvization and worked like a charm. J Company started firing, the Argentinians replied with everything they had, up went the illumination shells, in went the MILAN rockets, and heavy-machine-gun post after heavy-machine-gun post disappeared in fragments. Meanwhile, K and L Companies were also attacking Mount Harriet – but from a totally unexpected direction. Here again, they fought the classic 'thinking Marine's battle' – no senseless charging, taking their time to work out how to destroy an enemy position and then doing so with tremendous speed and aggression.

'The thing I'll always remember about Royal down South,' said one of the navy attached personnel, 'was coming across the lads in 42 one day, up in the mountains, sitting down and having a laugh and a joke with their CO. And it was absolutely pissing down and freezing cold. No one liked it, of course – but it wasn't the CO's fault and it wasn't the brigadier's fault that the weather was so lousy – so why bitch about it? They just took whatever was thrown at them and went on and did their job.'

When the Falklands had been won and the British forces were on their way home, a check was made on the Royal Marines who had been up in the mountains. It was found that in each unit, between seventy-five and ninety per cent of all men had developed trench foot to a greater or lesser extent. Trench foot is one of the most painful injuries imaginable . . . the Royal Marines had proved once again that it's the ability to endure that wins battles as much as anything else.

'The major mistake we made,' said a senior Royal Navy officer, 'was in thinking that the Guards were Royal Marines – that they'd been trained up to a similar standard.'

Quite why the Welsh and Scots Guards were sent to the Falklands in the first place remains something of a mystery. For while it could have been – and is – justified on the ground that they were part of Britain's reserve forces, earmarked for just such an occasion, the suspicion still remains that someone, somewhere, decided that should any glory result from the Falklands War, then the Guards should share in it.

Either way, it was a desperately unfair decision to make – unfair not only to the Paras and Marines who were forced to share the brunt of the fighting, but to the Guardsmen themselves, particularly those who died.

The two main problems were that the Guards had not been trained for amphibious warfare and they were not, frankly, fit enough for the type of campaign the Falklands demanded. Given their own choice, many Marines would much rather have seen a regiment like the Green Jackets (specialist light infantry, trained for fast, foot-mobile operations) or a solid county regiment like the Royal Anglians accompany themselves and the Paras into battle. For, aside from anything else, the Guards were primarily trained for warfare in central Europe, a type of campaign which depends on motor transport – is, in fact, mechanized to the nth degree. No such campaign or equipment was possible or available in the Falklands – a fact

Argentinians from 602
Commando Company,
survivors of the raid on Top
Malo, under guard by a member
of the Cadre.
Right: An Argentinian sniper
killed by 42 Commando on
Mount Harriet

that had to be brought to the attention of 5 Infantry Brigades' staff officers when they produced a plan of advance that would have made much sense on the plains of Germany, but was totally impractical on East Falkland.

There was, too, another problem that still exists in certain areas of the British armed forces, but is usually glossed over at best, ignored at worst. And that is the dividing line between officers and senior NCO's. To understand this it's necessary to know a little about certain traditional approaches to military line of command.

As we've seen, in the Royal Marines – and indeed the Paras – NCOs act as the middle management. Young officers are still learning their job, so much of the day-to-day running of a troop is the responsibility of the troop sergeant. No one feels too upset about this, or put out. It doesn't affect discipline, and ultimately results in a far better officer, if only for the type of roles both the Marines and the Paras undertake. But that is a very British, a very 'commando' or special forces attitude and has not spread uniformly throughout the British Army – or, indeed, the RAF.

For there is another tradition that springs from the Prussian military system of line management. In this system, a young troop officer totally controls his men, is one hundred per cent responsible for everything. In other words, he effectively fulfils a good part of the role of his troop sergeant. It's a very great responsibility to put on the shoulders of a young man; and even if it works, it results in a great divide between officer and senior NCO, not to mention officer and men.

The USMC have a similar system (the American armed forces were, by and large, developed on the Prussian model, which accounts for the rather strange discipline of West Point) and as a result, have not in the main developed senior NCOs to the same standard as have the Royal Marines. For no matter how good the USMC senior NCO may be, he is not encouraged to take the same responsibility as is a Royal Marine sergeant – why should he, runs the argument, when there is a young lieutenant equally capable of doing the job?

But that young lieutenant is not always capable of doing the job – how can he, when he lacks so much experience? Not only that, but such a system was predicated originally on the class and education divide that nowadays is – or should be – a thing of the past. Not so much for democratic reasons, but because today's soldier must be better educated, must be capable of more initiative than even his Korean War counterparts in order to survive on the battlefield.

The Guards still tend to cling to the established system. While it may make good sense in terms of their own traditions and military duties, it has little or no place in the type of campaign waged 'down South'. It affected their abilities to integrate with 3 Commando Brigade; overall, it affected their ability to *fight* alongside 3 Commando Brigade.

'I'll never forget,' said a Royal Marine, 'looking down from the mountains and seeing exactly where the Welsh Guards were. It was night, and you could see their cooking fires spread all over the countryside.'

Admittedly, the Guards at this time were not actually in the front line. But they were vulnerable to night attacks from snipers or aircraft, or even artillery moved forward from Port Stanley. And while it may seem a small thing to the uninitiated, it does bring home, to those who know, the

14 June 1982 and 45
Commando set off on their
historic yomp towards Port
Stanley

tremendous gap in fieldcraft between the Guards on the one hand, and the Marines and Paras on the other – and the lack of plain common sense shown at a very basic level. For if you do not encourage initiative at a junior level, if you make someone else responsible for taking all the decisions, then no matter how high the quality of the men themselves, they will not think for themselves. Why should they, when it's both discouraged and pointless anyway?

This is not to take anything away from the bravery shown by Welsh and Scots Guards alike. Nor is it intended as a criticism of any individual – except, perhaps, those individuals responsible for sending the Guards to the Falklands in the first instance. It is a criticism of a system that results in such a marked divide between officers and men, between officers and senior NCOs and, indeed, between the Brigade of Guards and the rest of the armed forces.

'There's no question,' said a Royal Marine who had been in a position to know, 'that Guards NCOs would be bloody good at their job, if they were allowed. Thing is, they're kept in total ignorance of what's happening by their officers. One of the saddest things was talking to the guys who'd been caught on the *Galahad* and learning that they just hadn't known what was going on.'

Knowing the enemy

Rumours have begun to circulate about Argentinians being killed after they had surrendered. This is how it happened:

British forces would fight forward against Argentinian fortified positions. As they advanced, at least one Argentinian trench would fly a white flag. This would be ignored, as bitter experience taught that a white flag simply meant that a single trench – often a single man in a single trench – had surrendered, and that the other Argentinians did not consider that white flag binding on the rest of them. Not even for the few minutes it would take to clear up the matter.

Again, the Argentinian forces had an unfortunate tendency to fight until the very last moment, trying to kill as many British troops as they could, until their opponents were literally at the edge of their trenches. At which point they would immediately try to give up – would either throw their hands in the air, or cower at the bottom of the trench. Too little too late, and very few survived.

You cannot expect a man to suddenly rein in his aggressions, particularly in the confusion of a firefight, particularly if that firefight was at night as so many were. And when you think about it, the Argentinian attitude was either incomprehensibly naive – or totally arrogant. In effect they were saying 'It's okay for us to kill as many of you as we can, but the moment we can't kill any more, you must stop trying to kill us.' That, with a little admixture of Latin pride that demands a man make a gesture before giving in – never mind that the gesture involved the killing of other people.

War is not a place for immature, adolescent fantasies. It is a place where each man is judged by his actions, not his intentions. And the moral for any future enemy of this country is that the time to surrender to the Royal Marines or the Paras is before you kill any of them, not afterwards. Either that, or run away.

But if the Royal Marines were effective in the Falklands, they were and still are doubly so in Northern Ireland. However, it's difficult to write about Northern Ireland from an operational point of view since the 'war' still continues – and it would be wrong to mention a particular tactic or method of operating that would lessen the Marines' effectiveness or possibly result in someone getting killed or injured. Having said that, it is perhaps possible to give some idea of why the Marines have done so well in Northern Ireland – depending, of course, on your point of view.

As with any long-drawn-out war (and it *is* a war in Northern Ireland, make no mistake about it) it's easy to become demoralized after a period of time. Easy for the British forces, that is, who find themselves unable to conduct the war in the way they'd like – and who see very little chance of it ending in the foreseeable future. This has, understandably, resulted in some units going to Northern Ireland with a slight feeling that they should really just keep their heads down for the duration – not take too many unnecessary risks. Other units, possibly as a counter to this, measure their own success in terms of how many incidents occurred and were dealt with. The Royal Marines would take a slightly different approach. First they believe in totally dominating the area they're assigned to. Second, they'll know that they have achieved this domination when no further incidents occur – no kneecappings, no assassinations. Obviously it doesn't always happen that way. But over the years the various terrorist organizations have developed a grudging respect for the Marines – and for the Marines' propensity to fight in Northern Ireland as they would in any other theatre of war: cautiously, aggressively, with a high degree of imagination and rough good humour.

'I remember once when I was a corporal,' reminisced a senior NCO, 'and I was taking my section down this road at night when someone took a shot at me. Missed by miles as a matter of fact, but still the first thing I did was shoot out all the streetlights with my SMG [sub-machine gun]. Now the civil authorities had got very upset about streetlights being shot out, and some idiot had issued orders that this wasn't to happen again. Well, I ask you – what would you do out in the open with a sniper around – pose for the bastard? Anyway, tinkle, tinkle out go the lights and we take up defensive positions in the dark. Nothing happens, so I figure the guy's buggered off and we carry on patrolling.

'Next night I took my section into one of the local clubs. We were pretty sure that the gunman, whoever he was, would be there or at least drink there regularly. So we burst in – bit Wild West really – and I stood there in front of my section and said: "One of you bastards took a shot at me last night!"

'As you can imagine, there's a chorus of "No, wasn't anyone from here" . . . "Ah, you've made a mistake" . . . "No one from here'd do a thing like that." But I knew they were lying and they knew I knew, so I said:

' "Not only that, but whoever did it was a terrible shot. I don't know what's wrong with you fellows – all those guns and ammunition you've got, why don't you spend some time down in the Republic learning how to shoot properly? You should be ashamed of yourselves – call yourselves gunmen?"

'Okay, that might seem all a bit macho, but what I was really doing was:

Where no prospect pleases – on patrol in Armagh

155

Top: Adopting the Marines'
standard triangular defensive
position, a four-man patrol
establishes radio contact with
HQ

Bottom: Searching for mines or
booby traps requires skill,
imagination and a high degree
of courage

Opposite above: Northern
Ireland is also a sniper's war.
Here one of the most successful
snipers settles to his task

Opposite below: Inside the
Drummuckavall observation
post (OP), used by 45
Commando in South Armagh.
Overlooking the border, this OP
was constantly under mortar
attack

a) telling them I knew they'd been involved, b) telling them we weren't scared, and c) throwing it right back in their faces. Not challenging them, mind – just letting them know that we were boss. So we went to leave, and suddenly there's another chorus of remarks. Only this time they were saying "We'll get you next time!" But they never did – maybe because they knew my guys would've been through that club like a dose of salts if they'd tried anything again.'

Royal Marines invariably bring their own brand of unorthodoxy to Northern Ireland, often with slightly surprising results. One time, a patrol came across an attempted rape. The sergeant in charge recognized the girl as the daughter of one of the local IRA godfathers. His men were all for dropping the would-be rapist from a second-storey window a few times, before turning him over to the police. But the sergeant ordered them to let

him go – which they did, having first established his identity. Then, with the girl in tow, they set off for the pub where her father could usually be found.

'It was,' said one of the Marines who had been present, 'the kind of pub where you had to walk in and immediately cock your weapon, otherwise someone would shoot you. So we did, and there was the girl's father looking daggers at us. So the sergeant walked up to him and explained what had happened – that this bloke had tried to rape the man's daughter and we'd stopped him. The daughter told her old man it was all true, and we left. As we went out the door, a voice said: "Thanks, Royal. We won't forget."

'And they didn't – the rest of our tour there was the quietest we'd ever known it. As for the rapist? Oh, he was found floating in some canal or other a week or so later. Crazy kind of war, though – that girl's father would probably be happy to shoot anyone of us on our next tour there.'

Undoubtedly much of the Marines' success in Northern Ireland has been due to the deadly efficiency of their snipers. Royal Marine snipers are used not only to kill known terrorists, but also to gather intelligence using cameras and microphones. They're usually inserted into their hide – which can be anything from a two-foot crawl space between floors to a conveniently placed pile of coal – under cover of darkness and as part of a standing patrol. And there they'll stay, often for days at a time, until they've achieved their objective. This can be something as seemingly mundane as a photograph proving that a shot terrorist was in fact carrying a weapon at the time. For the moment that a terrorist is shot, on the streets, there is a frantic effort made to get the weapon away – an effort that often involves the use of children. This isn't because the terrorist groups are particularly short of weapons, but because the accusation can then be made that British forces have shot an unarmed man.

Sniping is a solitary task, even though a sniper will work with a number-two man whenever he can – someone to provide him with some measure of protection.

Snipers are known for their slightly sardonic sense of humour. One story tells about the sniper who had been inserted into his hide with a rifle he was using for the first time. As luck would have it, he was able to shoot a known terrorist armed with a gun – the unfortunate man walked round the wrong corner at the wrong time. The sniper called up for a team to get him out. When they arrived, they all walked towards where the body of the terrorist still lay on the pavement, a bullet wound over one eye.

'Good shot,' said one of the Marines.

The sniper merely grunted, took a closer look at the body and readjusted his sights. For a facing head shot, snipers aim at a point between the eyes. He'd been out by two inches.

The last word

Perhaps the last word on Northern Ireland should be left to a Royal Marine who has, if nothing else, a novel explanation for much of the trouble there. A senior NCO, he was first out in Northern Ireland some fifteen years ago, and has seen the situation change quite dramatically.

'When Royal first went over, we never took the kids – the ones who were always demonstrating – that seriously. The hard men, yes – but they were only a very very small minority. What would happen is that we'd see a crowd of teenage boys shouting and throwing things at us, and we'd pile into them – give the little buggers a few well-aimed smacks about the head and send 'em home to their mothers. Good crowd control because aside from anything else, it breaks the trouble up before it can start. See, I always figured that most of the reason why the young kids were getting involved was to look good in front of the girls. You know, be a hero and get to snuggle down in the back row of the stalls. So if you recognize that they're not hardened terrorists, and don't treat them as such, treat them as naughty little boys, then you take a lot of the wind out of their sails. But once you take them seriously, then you've got problems – they graduate to all sorts of nastiness. And women still play a big part, too: it's funny how it's no sin for a good Catholic girl to sleep with one of the gunmen. And the gunmen do get their pick of the girls, no doubt about it. Okay, you do have some real hard-line political bastards operating there. You always did. But you've also got people who are basically thugs, just in it for the money, the women and the glory. I can't help wondering if maybe we haven't pushed those blokes into being thugs by taking them at their own face value – that we haven't helped turn them into heroes.

'See, nowadays you get a crowd of teenagers cursing and swearing at you, and it's almost a full-blown military situation. Okay, it might be a set-up with terrorist snipers waiting to take you out. Even so, I do think that there are times when a judicial boot up the arse would do wonders. But we're not allowed to do that any longer. We've become more and more divorced from the people over there. It's not that you'd choose to have any of them as your best friend, but we've more and more become the occupying force they're always accusing us of being. What the hell – if I walk down the street at home and some little toe-rag insults me, I'll belt him. I don't really see why I shouldn't be able to do the same thing in Northern Ireland. But the authorities are so terrified of us being accused of brutality, it's "hands off". And it hasn't worked – we still get accused of every sin known to man when we're on tour over there.

'You know what our real frustration is over there? It's that we – and I mean the Brit forces now – could finish that situation off in weeks. But the politicians won't let us – too many special interests involved. And we wouldn't have to kill half the population either, or even a fraction of it. You see, we're trained to take the initiative, to *act* not *react* all the time. It's difficult to do that with a bunch of politicians breathing down your neck who often seem to be more worried about what the press is going to say that actually getting the job done.'

Or perhaps the last word should be the comment of a Royal Marines officer who walked into an RUC police station somewhere near the border and saw two charts on the wall. One was of the local IRA/PIRA organization, and had names and photographs. The other was of the local Loyalist organization, and had nothing.

'Tell you what,' said the Royal Marine, 'why don't you put all your own photos and names up on the Loyalist chart – it'll be just as accurate as the one you've got for the Provos.'

The RUC were not amused.

10/THE FEMININE ANGLE

Very few Royal Marines could finish their initial training at Lympstone without the support of their families. Similarly, very few Royal Marines could carry on with their job without the support of their wives. And just as it takes someone out of the ordinary to be a Royal Marine, so too are their wives really rather special

One of the Corps clichés is that Royal Marines tend to marry nurses or teachers. Like most clichés, it contains more than a grain of truth.

'I suppose the reason is that nurses and Royal Marines have a similar sense of humour,' said one woman, herself a nurse and married to a Royal Marine sergeant. 'Plus they're both used to coping with enormous pressure, so they've got a lot in common.'

Another possible reason occurs – that the jobs of a Royal Marine, or a nurse or a teacher, all require some sense of vocation, of service. Certainly most women married to Royal Marines tend to be far removed from the stereotyped domestic, regimented, dependent service wife – a semi-fictitious character in any event.

Most women married to Royal Marines show a refreshing independence. Most pursue their own careers and have a far greater say in the running of the household, have far greater responsibility within the relationship than most of their civilian sisters – if only because of the amount of time their husands spend away.

'I had to deal with selling and buying a new home, and arrange the move all on my own,' remembers one wife, 'and I'm sure that in the early years of our marriage I knew more about handling domestic problems than my husband did – things like mending plugs and fixing a leaking pipe.'

Sudden responsibility can come as a shock. As another woman said: 'The very day we were due to move to our new house, he was sent off to the Falklands. And that was very shortly after we were married. I'd always lived with my parents before – very cosy and safe – and suddenly I had to cope with my husband disappearing and the move to a new home, and it was a bit difficult. But I think it was good for me, it made me far more self-sufficient.'

The Corps encourages Marines to buy their own houses – there are fewer married quarters available than in the Army, and wives cannot normally accompany their husbands on a posting of a year or less. This, plus the Corps' overseas training commitments, does result in a great deal of separation, and encourages wives to develop their own careers – as well as encouraging Royal Marines to look for wives who will be able to cope on their own.

One woman had been very impressed that her husband had been prepared to leave the Corps because he hadn't wanted to subject her to the pressures of separation when they were first married. But after thinking about it, she'd decided that since the job was so important to her husband and – since she agreed with what he did – it would be totally unfair to ask him to quit.

Which raises the question of how much do wives understand about their husbands' jobs? Much of what the Royal Marines do is classified. Nor do Royal Marines as a body particularly enjoy taking their work home with them. But they are aware that leaving families in total ignorance can have an absolutely devastating effect.

'The policy in this branch,' explained a member of the SBS – one of the most necessarily secret organizations in Britain, 'is that we should tell our wives as much as we possibly can without breaching security. We do try to involve them in our work, as much as they want to be involved and as much as we legitimately can.'

However, not every Marine is in the SBS – and the fact that they are both trained for and capable of legitimate violence is not always immediately apparent within a relationship.

'All the Royal Marines I know are really gentle, caring people at home. They never go over the top, as you might expect.'

'I look at my husband sometimes, when he's bimbling around the house, and think, "Can you really be a Royal Marine, you're just so relaxed – how can you do your job!" He'll switch on the aggression sometimes, usually when he's talking to an insurance salesman, but mostly he's just very quiet, very content to stay in the house.'

'One of the biggest shocks I ever had in our marriage was when I drove him up to his unit when he was leaving for Northern Ireland – and suddenly I saw him with a gun in his hand for the very first time. That's when it really struck home. I knew about it in theory of course, but that side of his life is something you try not to think too much about because if you do you'll begin to worry about him.'

'Yes, of course I've thought about the possibility of him killing someone, specially when he was in the Falklands. All I can say, if it's a choice between him and the other guy, I only hope it's him.'

Royal Marines themselves, particularly the men and NCOs, tend to be more intelligent and better educated than their army equivalents. Their wives reflect this fact, which has resulted in a lessening of the traditional class barriers between wives of officers and other ranks. But not altogether.

'I think the problem is that many of the women don't actually know how to behave with one another,' said one highly successful (working) wife of a Royal Marine senior NCO, 'and so you get a degree of snobbery that the men themselves don't show. It's all very silly really, but I do think that if there's a problem it's more of the wives' own making.'

Another wife of a senior NCO said that she'd found far more snobbery in the sergeants' mess than she ever had from officers' wives:

'I went to two major functions there and then told my husband "never again". Too many women sitting around claiming that they were better than someone else, for whatever reason. I don't know why they should be like that – I only know I don't want to be involved. But on the whole I find that outside the mess, all the wives take you pretty much as they find you. Not that I know many – a few in my husband's own branch, a few married to his close friends. But because we've got our own house and live some distance away from his work, most of our friends are civilians, most of mine are from work.'

This attitude runs very strongly counter to traditional military practice, which saw the families of a soldier effectively as part of the same regiment or corps, to the extent that wives often appeared to be given the same (honorary) rank as their husbands – and were expected to take part in the regimental life. Yet it appears to be the norm nowadays that wives not only don't want to be treated in that way, but that their husbands prefer a complete separation of job and family: they need an antidote to the highly pressurized, intensely masculine life that they lead when on duty.

'The nice thing is,' said the wife of an officer, 'that they don't seem to have to prove themselves at home, don't have to strut around saying "I'm a big tough Marine", because of course they've already proved how tough they are in their training. If you look in our village on a Saturday morning, you'll find that most of the men who are out shopping with their wives or pushing a pram are Royal Marines. I notice that my husband seems to enjoy the simple domestic things – like going shopping.'

But not all is sweetness and light, particularly when the men have to go away. Fairly obviously, the problem times are just before and just after a trip.

'It's always the same. We know he'll be going away for a month or even longer, and we tell each other we'll have a really nice few days before he goes off. But it never happens that way – we find ourselves snapping at each other, both becoming very tense. So we never do get to have those candlelit farewell dinners!'

'I find that just before he's off I get very edgy and lose my temper for no apparent reason. We've both got used to the idea that we'll have at least one major row before he goes. I think it's as much due to the anxiety I'm feeling as anything else. After he's gone, the first two weeks are the worst, and then you get into your own routine and life gets back to normal.'

Returning home brings its own problems.

'Of course you're pleased to see him come home. But you've also established your own way of doing things and you frankly resent this other person who demands to be considered too! The biggest thing with me is meal times. I never have set ones when I'm on my own, except when the children are home, but he insists that we do!'

'Dirty laundry. Suddenly there's piles of it scattered around, bits of military kit that he hasn't got round to cleaning yet.'

'I find that I also have to remind him to be considerate to his family when he's been away for any great length of time. We'll be out for a walk with the children and he'll be striding off in front, and I have to say: "Look, remember they're still very small and can't actually keep up." Mind you, I'm not saying that he wouldn't set off at a near run anyway. It's just that that lack of thought is more marked when he's been away for

Right: *Canberra*'s triumphant return with (opposite) the balloons going up

any length of time. It takes him a few weeks to adapt to us as individuals again.'

A series of absences obviously has some effect on the role of the man as the head of the household. It seems that Royal Marines – and possibly many other service marriages – concur far more with the partnership ideal than many civilian relationships. As one wife put it:

'I suppose he is "head of the household" in one sense – but there's never any question of suddenly reasserting his authority when he gets back home. He's quite happy to let me go on making the decisions I've done in the past. In fact, he won't let me push any of them on to him, says it's good for me to carry on as before. All he – and most of his friends – appear to want to do when they get back is just become involved. In a way, it would be easier if they did take over completely, because then you wouldn't have to continually remind yourself that there's another person involved and that you *should* discuss things with them, no matter how well you've coped when they haven't been there. Of course, there are some wives who just never cope when their husbands are away. You hear stories about some women suffering breakdowns. But how much of that is due to the increased responsibility, and how much to just worrying about them, I don't know. Personally, I can usually handle any separation up to three months. After that I begin to ask myself have I really got a husband, or is he a figment of my imagination?'

Long separations also call for a high degree of trust from husband and wife alike, particularly since Royal Marines don't spend all their time away in a theatre of war like the Falklands or Northern Ireland.

'You have to learn to trust one another,' explained one woman, 'because if you didn't, the marriage couldn't work. Oh, I'll go out with friends and enjoy myself when he's not here, but I'd never dream of having an affair. I don't want to, aside from anything else. But that element of trust is absolutely vital, on both sides. We couldn't exist without it.'

The picture that begins to build up is of a relationship that exists almost

independently of the husband's job. One wife said that she felt it was unhealthy for both husband and wife to be too strongly wrapped up in the same organization – if for no other reason than that the husband will find it all the more traumatic when he retires. She thought that a family life away from the Corps would help him make the inevitable adjustment to civilian life much more easily. However, it's not quite that simple. Even the most independent wives are aware of the fact that the Corps is there, as a potential cushion, and can take comfort in the fact. As one said:

'I suppose it is always nice to know that if you do have any problem, there's always someone who'll come round and help. And I do think that the Corps looks after, or cares, more about the families than a lot of other services. But on the other hand, I think too much of that can be a bad thing, makes not only the man but also his wife too dependent. I tell some of the guys that they don't know how spoilt they are – if they live in the mess, they never have to worry about a thing, everything's taken care of for them.'

The other part of the picture is that the wife is largely responsible for developing and maintaining the family unit. She has to compensate for the fact that her husband may miss a good part of the growing up of their children. In effect, she often becomes both father and mother – but has to be able to help her husband take over the father's role when he's at home. In some ways, the father's absences appear to affect daughters the most. Sons usually find it far easier to identify with their father's job, to gain vicarious pleasure from the fact that he's doing so many things that they themselves would like to do. But daughters may find it more difficult to appreciate the fact that their father's a soldier, doing something that they will never be able to do themselves.

And as an extremely personal observation, it might be that this is the reason why many service fathers make such an effort to get close to their daughters – even more so than to their sons. It's not that they don't love their sons, simply that they're aware that their daughters find it more difficult to comprehend and identify with their father's job.

The divorce rate is as high in the Royal Marines as it is elsewhere, possibly a little higher. But for the most part it appears to affect those marriages made when the man himself was still comparatively young – not long out of training – and when the woman herself was correspondingly young: neither totally aware of how difficult it is to be married to a Royal Marine, because of the separations, because of the demands of the job. Besides, not all Marines marry nurses or teachers and it appears to be difficult for many young women to comprehend or appreciate the dedication required to be a Royal Marine. They feel, perhaps naturally, perhaps not, that all a husband's energies should be focused upon his wife and family. Certainly those women, married in their mid twenties and beyond to Royal Marines who had been in the Corps for several years, were struck by the way their husbands-to-be explained exactly how difficult being married to a Royal Marine would be – that no attempt was made to gloss over the problems. It is almost as if Royal Marines decide to get married, and then search for a woman who they think will be able to cope – that the need is as much for a domestic environment as it is for the 'one, true love' in their life.

Certainly those marriages that work appear to do so extremely well. And in spite of their independence, many wives positively enjoy the very 'Royal Marinish' aspects of their husbands' characters – even down to the unique slang that Marines talk.

'I don't think I understood one word in three when we first met,' remembered one wife, 'and it took me some time to get used to words like "scran", "drip", "proff", "threaders" and all their other little expressions. Now I don't give it a moment's thought, often find myself using the same slang when I'm at work – much to the surprise of the people I work with.'

The one thing that all wives have to do is get used to the sardonic Marine sense of humour. It was characterized by one woman as the ability to laugh at anything, including themselves. Another woman said that she still found it a little bit too savage, even hurtful on occasions. But by and large she'd learnt not to fall for the bite, the deliberate wind-up, which only works if the recipient reacts to it.

But ask them what qualities make their husbands unique in their wives' eyes, and most women find it difficult to express their feelings.

'I think that if you walk into any room, you can usually tell who's the serviceman there,' said one, 'and not just because he's the one with the short hair. It's something about him – more relaxed, more confident perhaps, more at ease with everyone. Well, Marines are like that, but more so.'

'They are an elite force,' explained another woman, 'and I know that because my husband's always telling me so! But seriously, they do have this sense that they're that much better than other soldiers – better trained, better able to look after themselves, better able to do the job – and I suppose this confidence just shows through.'

'To me it's that he's always so relaxed about everything, to the point that he won't argue or quarrel about trivial things – nor will I, for that matter, because we don't have that much time together as it is.'

'I think it's just that he can get on with absolutely everyone, doesn't matter who they are.'

'You always hear about macho Marines, but honestly I don't think I've ever met more than two who thought they were God's gift – and you'll always get one bad apple. If anything, the surprising thing about my husband is that he is so quiet. But at the end of the day you are aware that he *is* a little bit special – and God forbid that I should be married to a nine-to-five bank clerk – can't imagine anything more boring.'

'I suppose the thing is, I'm aware that no matter how laid-back he appears, he always likes to feel independent and in control. He doesn't miss very much, you know.'

The sum of all this appears to be that the wives of Royal Marines, like Royal Marines themselves, are 'naturals' for the job.

What is true is that Royal Marines themselves couldn't operate a fraction as efficiently as they do without the support of their wives and families. Which is probably why so many Royal Marines asked that, if this book were to be dedicated to anyone, it should be to their wives – a very welcome sentiment, even if it does disagree with received wisdom about combative soldiers and their docile wives.

11/EAST OF SUEZ

Royal Marines in the Far East, in the jungle and at sea – and some indication of how they differ in operational effectiveness from the United States Marine Corps

The USMC gunnery sergeant had been happily surprised to discover how similar his own corps was to the Royal Marines. Sent as an observer to Bravo Company, 40 Commando Royal Marines, as they trained in jungle warfare in Brunei, he'd been struck by the similarity of many Royal Marine techniques to those practised by the USMC – but with the proviso that the Royal Marine techniques were perhaps a little too basic.

For example, 'harbouring-up' techniques are amongst the most vital practised by any military formation in the jungle. They're used when a unit establishes camp for the night or a permanent or semi-permanent camp by day. The Royal Marines always try to work on the principle of a triangular perimeter, with a fire-support team at each angle and the headquarters somewhere in the middle. The first fire-support unit moves in to secure the perimeter's apex, then the other two teams secure the two base positions, always one at a time so that two teams can cover the one moving. A similar technique is used, say, for river crossings. First one team will cross, supported by the two on the original river bank. Then one more crosses, and the two teams set up the base of a pyramid. Then comes headquarters (if there is one), finally followed by the third fire-support team who will complete the triangle's perimeter. Then, having established via scouts that the area is safe, the entire unit will move out. By and large, this triangular technique holds good for all Royal Marine formations in the jungle, from section to full-company level – although the Royal Marines would be loath to move a full company in the jungle as this invariably causes problems. This demonstrates the Corps' belief that in order to fight successfully – and survive – in the jungle, you must follow that well-known Corps acronym KISS, otherwise known as Keep It Simple, Stupid.

The USMC on the other hand will use a variety of harbouring-up techniques, including an oval perimeter formation and one known as the doughnut – essentially two ovals one inside the other. But then, the USMC tends to operate in slightly larger fighting units than the Royal Marines, with subsequently greater firepower at its disposal. And often,

extra men and extra firepower don't so much allow for different tactics as dictate them.

The basic fighting unit within the Royal Marines is undoubtedly the ten-man section led by a corporal. That's ten in theory, because the section often numbers considerably less, which means that a tremendous amount of responsibility is given to and expected from a Royal Marine corporal – far more so than from his equivalent in the USMC, where the basic fighting unit tends to be the platoon, or troop, numbering at least thirty.

In part this is dictated by the sheer size of the USMC (although, proportionate to the population of the United States, the USMC is the same size as the Royal Marines) – a size that allows for wholesale battalion, regimental and divisional manoeuvring. The Royal Marines can usually expect no more than two Commandos (i.e. two battalions) to be deployed together, and then strung out over a large land area. Small wonder that the Royal Marines have had to develop the art of fighting in small units – as indeed has the British Army, although not to quite the same extent – tactics which are in any case more suited both to the modern battlefield and the Royal Marines' role as commando troops.

This difference between the USMC and the Royal Marines has also been partly dictated by the basic American belief that superior firepower will conquer all. It is a theory that was once described by a US military attaché in London as the 'wagon train' tactic, owing its origins to the old pioneer technique of closing ranks and bringing as much firepower as possible to bear on attacking Indian tribes. It is primarily defensive in nature and tends to assume that the enemy will always attack first. Translated into modern warfare – particularly jungle warfare – it explains the thirty man patrols that the American forces tended to use in Vietnam. (But not all American forces did this – their Long Range Reconnaissance Patrols, for example, borrowed and improved on tactics used by the British during the Malayan Emergency.)

However, the jungle warfare techniques the Royal Marines now teach are not based so much on the Malayan Emergency, or the Confrontation with Indonesia, as on the Australian and New Zealand experiences in Vietnam. It was generally accepted that the Australian contingent in Vietnam were amongst the most effective troops there. They used the four- or six-man-patrol technique: men going out into the jungle for weeks at a time (living off the land wherever possible), both to gather intelligence and to deny the ground to the Vietcong or the North Vietnamese Army (NVA). It was far harder for either the Vietcong or the NVA to discover such small patrols – which in turn were plenty large enough to mount hit-and-run ambushes at night, particularly on couriers or supply columns.

The point is that a pitched battle between large opposing forces in the jungle is often a waste of time. Visibility is at best fifteen metres, often only five. It's too easy to be either outmanoeuvred, or to discover that you've spent an hour or so pouring fire in on an enemy who simply isn't there. It's also far too easy for a large unit to be tied down by a much smaller enemy force. In other words, the best counter to guerrilla tactics is . . . guerrilla tactics. It is those tactics that the Royal Marines teach their men – and again, the only reason they're able to do so is because their basic fighting unit is so comparatively small.

None the less, reliance on technology does aid the USMC in one very important area – a Marine's personal equipment. To take one example, the USMC jungle boots – now happily on issue to selected British units – are vastly superior to the British-pattern jungle boot which even when it was first developed over twenty years ago, was nothing short of a disgrace. USMC tropical clothing is also better – strong but lightweight cotton – whereas the new British jungle camouflage suit contains a high percentage of nylon. Not only will this melt and meld to the skin in a fire, it also means that the man wearing it begins to smell of sweat after only a few hours. This might seem a small point, but in an environment where you often can't see three metres away, a man's smell is all that's needed to show you which patch of bush to blast with an SA80, an AR16 or a shotgun. Essentially, compared to the USMC, the Royal Marines in the jungle are at the same disadvantage as the USMC is in Norway and the Arctic – inadequate equipment that probably cost as much (if not more) as the right kit for the job.

It's in the jungle, too, that the basic difference between USMC and Royal Marine recruit training techniques shows itself. The USMC breaks a man down to rebuild him in its own image. The Royal Marine challenge – and help – a man to develop those abilities that will make him a compe-

tent rifleman in a troop – and all subsequent Royal Marine training is of the same pattern. It's almost brainwashing versus high-pressure education, and means that the young Royal Marine tends to be far more self-reliant (and with far more to say for himself) than his USMC equivalent. Far more is also expected of him in terms of initiative and self-discipline – and in the jungle especially, these qualities are invaluable.

Overall, the major difference between the USMC and the Royal Marines is their countries' different cultures. It's a great mistake to assume that a common language means a similar culture, a similar way of looking at things. It's often a source of puzzlement that a country like the United States, overall far less formal than Britain, should have developed a military system that relies so much on imposed discipline. It's particularly strange when you consider that the earliest military traditions in the US were those of commando-type formations – George Washington's sharp-shooters who played such havoc with British and German mercenary forces. In many ways today's USMC has as much, if not more, in common with the French Foreign Legion – a very formal, imposed discipline – than with the Royal Marines.

A world of difference

By way of a slight detour, there's another area which highlights one of the differences between US and British military thinking – the way each country uses its special forces. While the US Navy's SEAL (SEA Air Land) and UDT (Underwater Demolition Teams) are quite close in concept and activity to Britain's SBS and Royal Navy Clearance Divers,

there is a world of difference between the SAS and SBS on the one hand, and the US Special Forces on the other. It's a difference that goes as far back as the Second World War, and briefly it is this: US Special Forces are intended, where possible, to work closely with and train 'friendly' local forces, e.g. the Montignards in Vietnam, or the Resistance in Occupied France. The SAS and SBS are expected to operate as independently as possible, coming into contact with local resistance groups or potential allies only if absolutely necessary, or possibly for a one-off operation.

In many ways it's a contrast between extreme pragmatism on the one hand and idealism on the other. It's not that idealism is lacking in the British armed forces, merely that it has little or no place tactically. Nor would the SAS or SBS assume, because a local guerrilla force was fighting the same enemy, that they all shared the same motivations or objectives. With that, both the SAS and SBS always operate in conditions of extreme secrecy, in peacetime as well as war, and neither group is expected to be as regimental as, say, the Brigade of Guards. On the other hand, the US Special Forces appear to be expected to fulfil an unconventional role while looking, and operating, as conventional military forces – to the point that Pentagon-applied bullshit has on many occasions definitely baffled US Special Forces' brains. It may well be that the new independent US Special Forces' unified command will free its units to operate more effectively – but the thought still remains that until the Pentagon radically rethinks its approach to modern warfare, and realizes that image is less important than ability, it will not be able to develop its armed forces to their best potential.

40 Commando in Brunei. Using only their gollocks (jungle knives) plus available natural materials (rattan, bamboo etc.), each six-man section is given two hours to produce a basha, an animal trap, a rain water trap and to build a fire – which must be lighted with one match.
Left, below: An animal trap based on a sapling spring. Note improvised dagger blade, close to the front figure's right hand. It should have been rubbed with mud to disguise it – otherwise a skilful, lethal trap

Below: A good basha – sleeping platform at a good height; roof fairly rainproof. Right: Highly imaginative rain trap, and (right below) firewood and termite mounds – latter burned to keep mosquitoes away. (Dried cow pats will have same effect in temperate climates)

A Sea Rider (crew of two) off
Hong Kong

3 Raiding Squadron, Hong Kong

It's in Hong Kong that one can see just how effective the Royal Marines are in operating in very small, independent units – for example, 3 Raiding Squadron Royal Marines (some twenty officers and men).

Smuggling has always been a problem in Hong Kong – which is pretty apt since smuggling was really Hong Kong's original *raison d'être* – and the situation's no better today. The major problems are illegal immigrants from mainland China and North Vietnam; drugs into and out of the colony (Hong Kong tends to be used as a staging post, or entrepôt port, for much of the heroin originating in the Golden Triangle); and electrical goods, cigarettes, liquor, etc., into China. It has been argued that (apart from drugs) smuggling doesn't really hurt anyone. However, the smuggling is ninety per cent organized by the Triads, who could teach the Mafia a thing or two. Illegally imported electrical goods (or any goods) can play havoc with a country's economy; and the refugee problem is not as simple as it first appears. Aside from the fact that Hong Kong simply cannot absorb all the people who want to go there, many illegal immigrants are economic refugees pure and simple – particularly those from China, who tend to be male, aged between eighteen and twenty-four, and totally incapable of supporting themselves if they ever do reach Hong Kong. Often they're exploited as sweated labour on a building site, or they turn to crime. None the less, much of the illegal immigrant trade is reasonably 'sportingly' conducted – those immigrants who are caught and sent back often turn up again a month or so later – except for the problem of the children.

Many Chinese residents in Hong Kong have wives and families in China, and often try to have their children brought, illegally, into the colony. There is a waiting list of 100,000 children who could legally enter Hong Kong, and an estimated 200,000 waiting to be sent illegally. The going price for smuggling a child – some as young as eighteen months old – into the colony is Hong Kong $22,000, approximately £2,200 or US $3,500. Often the kids are drugged and hidden beneath the floorboards of sampans. On one occasion they were hidden beneath a pile of lobster pots – and two had died of suffocation by the time the boat was intercepted. The smugglers, known as 'snakeheads' (literal translation from the Chinese), aren't too fussed if one or two children out of a cargo of twenty or thirty are dead on arrival, even though terms are strictly cash on delivery from the parent waiting anxiously in Hong Kong. It's still a profitable run – and along with drugs, one of the dirtiest businesses in the world.

The illegal immigrant problem came to a head in 1979 when 90,000 flooded into the colony. It was decided to set up an experimental unit, operating from remote islands around Hong Kong, to detect and intercept snakeheads with their human cargoes. Within seven weeks 1,500 immigrants had been detained and 67 sampans impounded.

Thus 3 Raiding Squadron Royal Marines was born, and today it is mainly responsible for anti-smuggling patrols at night. It works in close co-ordination with the Hong Kong police and the Royal Navy – the latter using the new Peacock-class fast patrol craft plus single-engine Sea Rider inflatable boats. The Royal Navy operates by day and by night, usually independently of the Royal Marines, although the Peacock-class patrol craft can and are used as mother ships, particularly in thick fog, guiding the Royal Marines towards a suspect boat detected by radar.

Three Raiding Squadron's biggest asset, aside from the standard of its men (all from the Landing Craft Branch except for twelve local interpreters) is its Fast Patrol Craft. These were brought into service to counter the threat from the extremely fast speedboats that the snakeheads began using in 1983. FPCs are Rigid Inflatable Boats (RIBs) 8.1 metres in length and powered by twin 700 h.p. outboard motors. All the Marines will admit is that they are capable of a speed in excess of 38 knots. Anyone who's ridden in them could be forgiven for suspecting that they can go much, much faster than that – and riding in them is a memorable experience. For example, since they skim from one wave crest to another, the crew (usually two Marines and an interpreter) tend to bounce around a fair bit, even though they're sitting firmly on padded seats and can even strap themselves in. In a choppy sea – wave height three to four feet – it has been estimated that each crew member receives 5G every three seconds – that in one minute a man's body will have had a force five times the gravitational pull of the earth applied to it twenty times. Driving one of those monsters calls for immense skill and stoicism, since such continual pounding can and does result in injuries to the knees and back.

The Raiding Squadron also operates Sea Riders (with an admitted speed of 'up to 38 knots'), and a typical patrol, commanded by a corporal, may consist of one FPC plus two Sea Riders. The squadron varies its operating routines as much as possible, to confuse the snakeheads who continually

Above: 3 Raiding Squadron in action, boarding a suspect junk. (Try it at night in a heavy swell!)

Below: Somewhere in the South China Sea a RIB engine burns out (a plastic bag wrapped around the prop)

Above: More holes than planks – a mainland Chinese fishing sampan, routinely stopped and searched for contraband goods

Below: Royal Marine officer searching fish hold on a suspect junk. Two illegal immigrants were later found hiding in a cabin behind the bridge – trying to disguise themselves as folds in a duvet!

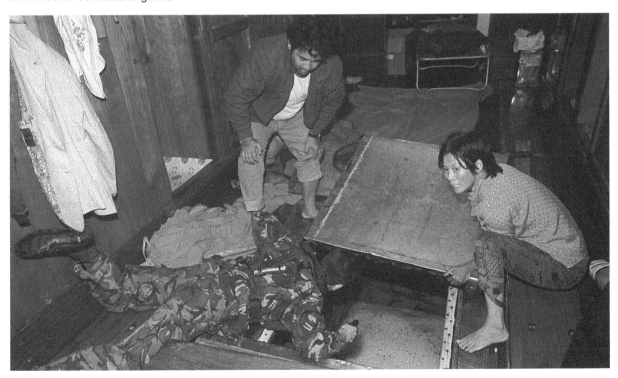

HMS *Swallow* (Peacock class
fast patrol ship) demonstrates
her skill at getting a Sea Rider
away within two minutes, South
China Sea. The Peacock class
ships in Hong Kong can and do
use their radar to direct 539
Squadron RM RIBs and Sea
Riders towards suspect
speedboats, sampans and
junks

ILLEGAL IMMIGRANTS

Illegal immigrants come into Hong Kong by a variety of methods:

– By land, by breaking through the border fence or simply by strolling across the
   no-man's-land of the border village of Sha Tau Kok.

– By sampan, which will hold up to forty immigrants.

– By floating, supported on an inflatable cushion.

– By swimming or walking across mud flats at low tide (these immigrants are
   known as 'mud skippers').

– By junks sailing out of Hong Kong or Macao, each holding up to one hundred
   immigrants. These junks usually stand offshore, and pick up and deliver their
   cargo of illegal immigrants by small dinghies equipped with solitary outboard
   engines.

Drug smugglers tend to use extremely fast speedboats, often powered by twin 800
h.p. outboard engines, capable of between 60 and 70 knots.

monitor the squadron's base at HMS *Tamar* on Hong Kong island. Each night, however, there are at least two separate patrols at sea, operating without lights and without radar, using only their navigational skills and local knowledge to guide them. They are in radio contact with each other and with the Hong Kong police, but the radio is used as little as possible because of the snakeheads listening in.

Squadron personnel must develop a good local knowledge. They have to know which speedboats are being used by the snakeheads at any one time – and which speedboats could be used for smuggling.

'We look for boats with extra-large fuel tanks,' explained a Marine, 'and those with hollowed-out interiors – everything stripped away to accommodate cargo. And then, you just get a feel for a boat or a skipper who's being a bit naughty.'

The patrols are empowered to stop any boat of any nationality within Hong Kong territorial waters. Obviously there's not a great deal of sense in stopping an ocean-going freighter, but they stop motorized or sailing junks many times the size of their FPCs or Sea Riders. They carry side arms (9mm automatic pistols) although as one Marine pointed out, the chances of hitting anything at high speed are pretty well non existent. Essentially, the weapons are carried in case the Marines are attacked once they've boarded a boat. In actual fact, there have been only two instances of the squadron being fired upon – and one turned out to be a genuine mistake. On 19 December 1982 a crew member on board a Chinese vessel loosed off a few rounds with an AK47, before being forcibly restrained by his own skipper. Many apologies later, it turned out that the crewman had thought his boat was being boarded by pirates (a justifiable concern since piracy is one of the major problems in the South China Sea) and that his skipper has been licensed by the Chinese government to carry eight rifles and 2,500 rounds of ammunition. The crewman had been concerned by the speed and efficiency with which the Royal Marines materialized out of the dark and boarded the vessel. The chances of such an accident happening again are remote, since by now the Raiding Squadron is well known in these waters. Not only that, but relationships – both official and unofficial – between the Squadron and their opposite numbers from the Chinese police are by and large excellent. On one other occasion four shots were fired at a night patrol on 14 April 1985 by a suspected speedboat smuggler – but the shots went well wide of their target. Generally speaking, if they're caught the snakeheads tend to give in gracefully – or with as good a grace as possible under the circumstances.

As can be imagined, anti-smuggling patrols mean that an awesome responsibility is vested in the patrol commander, a corporal – not only for the safety of his own men but also for the safety of illegal immigrants, since the snakeheads will often throw their passengers over the side, adults and children alike, in a bid to escape a pursuing patrol.

To return to the beginning of this chapter, it's almost inconceivable that such a responsibility would be vested in a corporal within the USMC. Or, to be honest, if it were vested, that he would be able to discharge his responsibilities to such good effect – not a reflection on the man himself, merely a comment about the military training and command techniques used by the United States.

ANNEX

PING THE BOOTIE – THE **ISH!**

ROYAL MARINE JARGON

Part of the mystique of the Royal Marines possibly derives from the fact that they speak a different language. It sounds like English; it even sounds frustratingly familiar – but is none the less totally incomprehensible to ninety per cent of the population in Britain, and only adds to the confusion when Royal goes abroad. Loosely based on Royal Navy slang, Royal Marinespeak comprises well over five hundred words and about half that number of phrases or expressions – which is a larger vocabulary than used by some recently discovered tribes in the interior of New Guinea. Thanks to the invaluable fieldwork conducted by Captain David Tong and Sergeant Rick Haynes (both Royal Marines), and thanks to the Corps magazine, *The Globe and Laurel*, here are just a few of the more common words and expressions used.

Ace	Good, excellent
Animal run	To really let one's hair down on a run ashore
Banjo	Broken down, as in 'banjoed'
Banyan	Picnic on a beach
Bimble	To wander around casually with one's mind in neutral
Bite	To be drawn into an argument; to accept an untruth
Bootneck/Bootie	Royal Marine. Possibly derived from the leather uniform stock worn around the neck during the Nelsonian era (USMC term 'leatherneck' may have same derivation)
Bombed out	Crazy
Boss	Respectful but casual way of referring to the officer in command
Brill/Brills	Brilliant, magnificent (pre-dates modern teenage slang by several decades)
Brammer	Outstandingly good
Bronzy	Sun tan
Bug-out	To conduct a military withdrawal
Buzz	A rumour; or a general description of the situation
Cheese-down	To laugh uncontrollably
Chuck one up	Salute
Cloggie	A Dutchman
Common dog	Common sense
Crab/Crab Air	Member of the RAF/the RAF
Crack	To achieve
Crappers	To be very drunk
Cream in	Collide
Crimbo	Yule-tide
Dig out (blind)	To make supreme effort
Dip-out/dip	To come off worse in any situation

Dischuffed	To take offence	**Prof**	a) To do well b) Legitimate perks
Drip	To complain	**Pussers**	Relating to anything (stores, equipment, regulations) to do with the Corps and/or Royal Navy. Anything done unimaginatively or by the book is done in a 'Pussers manner'
Drop a sprog	To give birth		
Earwigging	Eavesdropping		
Essence	Beautiful, usually applied to one's 'pash' or 'party'		
Flakers	Exhausted		
Foo foo	Talcum powder	**Puzzle palace**	Headquarters building
Gen	The truth	**Rice**	Effort
Glimp	To peer or peep	**Rock-all**	Nothing
Glop	To slurp or drink hurriedly	**Run ashore**	Rest and relaxation away from ship, barracks, office or camp
Glophead	A drunkard		
Goffer	a) wave b) cold drink c) punch	**Rock-ape**	Member of the Mountain Leader Branch; also member of the RAF Regiment
Gonk	To sleep		
Greenie	Saltwater wave	**Rug rat**	A baby
Grolly	Something unpleasant	**Sad-on**	Unhappy
Gronk	An unattractive woman	**SB**	Special Boat Squadron. One who joins the SBS is said to have 'gone SB'
Hand	Trustworthy, efficient man ('he's a good hand')		
Ickies	Money	**Scran**	Food
Ish (the)	To be equipped with everything possible; to be the best	**Shave off**	Expression of annoyance or to speak out of turn
		Shoot-through	Someone who fails an undertaking
Kag kaggage	Unwanted, useless equipment	**Skeg**	To observe or conduct a reconnaissance
Knacker/fat knacker	Someone unfit or overweight		
Limers	Soft drink with high vitamin C	**Skin**	Immature/inexperienced young man
Loopy looney juice	Alcohol	**Sneaky beaky**	Intelligence staff and their operations
Maskers	Masking tape. Invaluable to the Corps. When combined with a hammer is known as the 'Royal Marines tool kit'		
		Snurgle	Advance cautiously or crawl
		Sprog	Baby or anyone lacking experience
Mankey	Filthy		
Minging	a) Drunk b) Dirty	**Stacks**	Opposite of 'plums', especially in relation to success with women
Mod Plod	Ministry of Defence police		
Nause	Inconvenience	**Thin-out**	Depart
Nod/noddy	RM recruit	**Threaders**	Fed up
Nutty	Confectionery	**Trap**	To successfully attract a member of the opposite sex
Nutty fiend	Someone with a sweet tooth		
Party	A female	**Trough**	Eat
Pash	A female with whom a Royal Marine has formed a more than casual relationship. A fiancée	**Twitter**	Talk aimlessly
		Up homers	Invited into a home
		Up the line	Travel away from base
Percy pongo	A soldier in the Army. Derived from the RM belief that soldiers don't wash very often	**Wet**	A drink of any description
		Wrap	To stop or give up
		Yaffle	Eat hurriedly
Picturize	To give an explanation	**Yeti**	Spectacular fall on skis
Ping	Recognize or identify	**Yomp**	Force march with a heavy load
Piso	Careful with money	**Yo-yo**	Young officer under training at Lympstone
Plums	To gain nothing against expectations (see 'trap')		
		Zap	To shoot or be shot
Plums rating	Someone who's always unsuccessful with women	**Zeds**	Sleep

These examples of the records
kept on each recruit indicate
how closely every man is
evaluated at all stages of
training

PERSONAL QUALITIES

WKS OF TRG	MENTAL ABILITY	INITIA- TIVE	RELI- ABILITY	PHYS ABILITY	PROF ABILITY	GENERAL CONDUCT	UNSELF- ISHNESS	L/SHIP POTENTIAL	TOTAL
1 TO 15									
16 TO 24									
25 TO 30									
TOTALS									

*

NOTES:

1. Personal Qualities are to be graded as follows:

   5 - V GOOD; 4 - GOOD; 3 - AVE; 2 - BELOW AVE; 1 - POOR.

   However, in areas of doubt the following variations are acceptable:

   5 - 4.3 - V GOOD; 4.2 - 3.6 - ABOVE AVE; 3.5 - 2.6 - AVE; 2.5 - 1.8 - BELOW AVE; 1.8 - 0 - POOR.

2. Each reporting period is to be totalled at the end of the period. On completion of training final totals are to be calculated and the grand total entered in the box marked *.

FINAL ASSESSMENT GRADE

				SUBJECT
A	B	C	C-	

NOTES:

1. The Final Assessment grade is produced by totalling the figures recorded in boxes marked *. The boxes are at the end of training records for weeks 15 and 30 and for personal qualities at the end of training.

2. The gradings as related to this overall total are:

   A - 270 TO 235; B - 234 TO 195; C 194 TO 161; C- - 160 TO 140.

3. If a C- grading is awarded the specific subject area must be identified and expanded on in the box below.

TO BE COMPLETED IF A C- GRADE IS AWARDED

SUBJECT	DETAILS

TRAINING RECORD CARD

			JMNE/MNE		TROOP NO/S	

SURNAME & FORNAMES		SERVICE NO	D OF B		REL	B/G	

NEXT OF KIN & ADDRESS | RT | NAMET

T2

ENTRY DATE:
FIRST OPT-OUT DATE:
TEL NO: LAST OPT-OUT DATE:

CAREERS OFFICE	B'GROUND	EDUC	STAs	GP ACTS	ATT TO AUTH	L'SHIP	MOTIV	JOB RCD

OPT-OUT: REASONS GIVEN BY RECRUIT

PHYS	DISCIP	PERS ADMIN	H'SICK	PERS PROBS	UNSUITED	POOR PROSPECTS	NO IN-TEREST	RESTRIC-TIONS	OTHERS

PSO's COMMENTS:

NOT RECOMMENDED/RECOMMENDED: FOR RE-ENTRY TO: RM/OTHER SERVICES ONLY/ANY SERVICE
IN _____ MONTHS

END OF TRAINING REPORT:

PPs & SQ/TQ PREFERFNCES:
1.   2.   3.   4.

MEMORANDUM

To: Comdt   From: OC CTW

Date: 29 Oct 86   Ext: 202

Introduction

1   From 301 Troop which joined on 1 Sep 86 all the following Troops will be on the new Common Recruit Syllabus. A short guide to what is contained in each week is below.

2   CRS Outline Programme

Course
Week Detail
(a)   (b)

1   Join CTC/Attestation/Husbandry/Admin/ Medical/PT/PSO Interview/Issue Stores & Kit/Ex First Step

2   Lec's. General/Medical/Pay/PT Swimming. Clothing. X Rays and Audio's

3   Drill & Husbandry/PT Swimming/Lec's General/ Weapon Trg Rifle/RT

4   Weapon Trg Rifle/PT & Swimming/RT/1st Aid/ EX Twosome

5   Drill/PT/1st Aid/Swimming/Lec's General/Map Reading/Weapon Trg Rifle/RT/Signals

6   PT & Swimming/1st Aid/Drill/Trg Tests Rifle/ Intro Shoot & Grouping/Lec's General/Map Reading

7   Rifle Grouping/Zeroing/Elementary Application of Fire/Night Shoot/PT & Swimming/Drill/1st Aid/Map Reading/Signals

8   Drill/Kit Muster/Rounds/Ex Hunters Moon/Lec Corps History

9   PT & Swimming/Map Reading/Namet/Corps History

10   NBC/Rifle Shooting/Drill/PT/Signals/Survival/ Religion

11   Drill/PT/Map Reading/Mil Knowledge Test/Ex Omega Man/Dart Venture/Ryders Delight

12   Wpn Trg LSW/SMG/GPMG/Drill PT & Swimming/Medical/Clothing

13   Ex Baptist Run/Rifle PWT

14   Drill/Mil Knowledge Test/PT/R&I Trg/Map Reading

15   GPMG Intro Shoot/Namet/PT/Drill/Parents Day/ LWL

16   Change Coy's/PT/Lec's Tactics/Shooting Rifle/ LSW/GPMG

17   Signals/PT/Lec's Patrolling/Practical Patrolling/ Wpn Trg 66mm

18   PT/clothing/PSO Drafting/Lec's CRO/Corps History/Signals/Tactics/Map Reading/Lec/Demo OPs

19   Ex Silent Night

20   PT/Gren Lessons & Throwing/Wpn Trg 84mm & Shooting Sub Cal/Signals/Speed March

21   Lec & Practical Tactics/Speed March/Wpn Trg 66mm/FFX 1

22   Lec & Practical Tactics/FFX2

23   Kit Muster/NBC/Tactics/Clothing/Corps History/ BFT Passout/LWL

24   Lec's AE's/Ex Holdfast/RT/NBC

25   PT & Swimming/Speed March/Endurance Course/Helo Drills/Tactics/Unarmed Combat/ Drill/Signals

26   Bullet Pen Demo/Bayonet Fighting/PT/ Endurance Course/Lec: Practical Climbing/NI Navex/Lec: Practical FIBUA/Clothing/ Swimming

27   Visit Corp Museum/HMS *Victory*, SB Aquaint/ TT Coy Aquaint/Amph OPs Instructions/Ex Sea Sting/Nightmare

28   Ex Nightmare/PT/Endurance Course/Drill/Speed March/Clothing

29   Tzan Cse Passout/30 Miler/Lec's Pay&Security: Promotion: Current Affairs/Medical/Drill/ Unarmed Combat

30   Kings Squad/Admin

Rank/MAJ RM
Appt/OC CTW

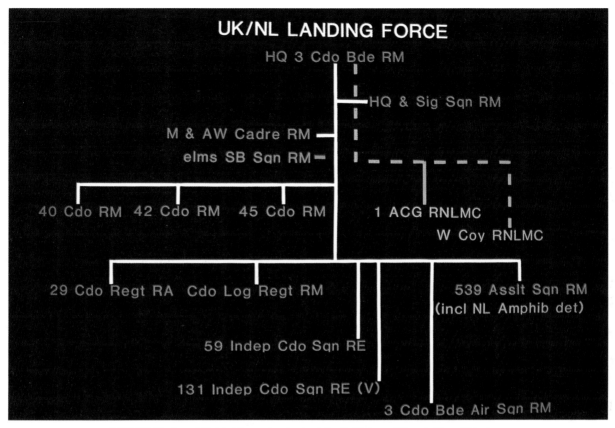

ORBAT (Order of Battle/Organization) of the British and Dutch Royal Marines
dedicated by NATO to the defence of Norway and thus the North Atlantic

WEAPONS USED BY 3 COMMANDO BRIGADE, RM

A Platoon Weapons
1 SLR – Self Loading Rifle
2 SA80 – IW and LSW – individual and light support
   weapon
3 GPMG – General purpose machine gun (light role
   and SF role)
4 LMG – Light Machine Gun – still employed in
   various theatres
5 9mm Browning Pistol
6 AR15 – (M16 used mainly by ML Cadres)
7 SMG – Sub Machine Gun (to be phased out), Stirling
8 2″ Mortar (being replaced by 51mm mortar)
9 66mm LAW – Light anti tank weapon
10 84mm MAW – Medium anti tank weapon
11 LAW 80 – Light anti tank weapon – will replace 9
   and 10
12 L42 Snipers Rifle
13 Heckler and Koch SMG } Special forces only
14 Ingram Machine Pistol }
15 Remington "Wingmaster" Shotgun – Certain
   Theatres only
16 Federal Riot gun – Internal Security only

B Grenades
1 L2 Grenade – HE
2 80 Grenade – Phosphorus

C Support/Heavy Weapons
1 81mm Mortar
2 Milan Anti tank Missile
3 Blowpipe Anti Aircraft missile – Now replaced by
   Javelin
4 105 Light Gun (29 Cdo Regt RA)
5 Rapier
6 Javelin – to replace Blowpipe
7 Stinger Anti Aircraft (RNLMC attached 3 Cdo Bde)
8 Dragon Anti Tank (RNLMC attached 3 Cdo Bde)
9 Lt/Med Recce Sqn (–) Scimitar 30mm cannon } Attached
                       Scorpion 76mm Gun   }

The three 'green-hatted' Royal Navy photographers who provided ninety per cent of the Falklands pictorial coverage to the world's press. Left to right: Al Campbell (Hasselblad and 7.62 SLR); Peter Holdgate (Nikon); Roger Ryan (Mamiya and 9mm SMG)

PHOTO ACKNOWLEDGEMENTS

Robin Adshead 76, 85, 136 (left, top & bottom), 168, 173, 176/177, 178, 180, 181 (bottom)

Audio Visuele Diest KM (RNLMC) 72/73, 74/75, 94/95, 98/99, 110/111, 113, 124/125, 140/141

Central Office of Information 56

FODOV 36/37, 38/39, 40/41, 44, 48/49, 52/53, 64/65, 67, 88, 93, 104 (left), 100 (right), 120/121, 128/129, 157 (top), 181 (top), 182

Peter Holdgate 2, 10, 14/15, 22/23, 28, 31, 47, 68/69, 70/71, 79, 80/81, 82, 89, 90/91, 100/101, 102, 104/105 (centre), 126/127, 131, 132, 134/135, 136/137 (top & bottom), 138/139, 142, 144/145, 146/147, 148/149, 150/151, 153, 154, 164/165, 170/171, 174, 175

Roger Ryan 1, 8/9, 12, 16/17, 18/19, 20/21, 24, 33, 60/61, 81 (inset), 86

Ministry of Defence 96, 116/117, 156, 157 (bottom), 160

Syndication International 54/55 (bottom)

Anthony Upton 26/27